T0293141

Occupational Labor Shortages

Occupational Labor Shortages

Concepts, Causes, Consequences, and Cures

Burt S. Barnow
John Trutko
Jaclyn Schede Piatak

2013

W.E. Upjohn Institute for Employment Research
Kalamazoo, Michigan

Library of Congress Cataloging-in-Publication Data

Barnow, Burt S.
  Occupational labor shortages : concepts, causes, consequences, and cures / Burt S.
Barnow, John Trutko, Jaclyn Schede Piatak.
    p. cm.
  Includes bibliographical references and index.
  ISBN-13: 978-0-88099-411-8 (pbk. : alk. paper)
  ISBN-10: 0-88099-411-8 (pbk. : alk. paper)
  ISBN-13: 978-0-88099-412-5 (hardcover : alk. paper)
  ISBN-10: 0-88099-412-6 (hardcover : alk. paper)
  1. Labor supply—United States. 2. Labor market—United States. 3. Occupations—
United States. I. Trutko, John W. II. Piatak, Jaclyn Schede. III. Title.
  HD5724.B337 2013
  331.13'60973—dc23
                               2012049811

© 2013
W.E. Upjohn Institute for Employment Research
300 S. Westnedge Avenue
Kalamazoo, Michigan 49007-4686

The facts presented in this study and the observations and viewpoints expressed are
the sole responsibility of the authors. They do not necessarily represent positions of
the W.E. Upjohn Institute for Employment Research.

Cover design by Alcorn Publication Design.
Index prepared by Diane Worden.
Printed in the United States of America.
Printed on recycled paper.

This book is dedicated to our spouses,
Joyce Kaiser, Deborah Trutko, and Michael Piatak.

Contents

Figures

Tables

Acknowledgments

The authors would like to thank the following individuals for sharing their time and expertise during interviews concerning the labor market conditions in the four occupations that were the focus of case studies included in this report: Erling E. Boe, University of Pennsylvania; Timothy Dall, The Lewin Group; Bruce M. Gans, Kessler Institute for Rehabilitation; Phoebe Gillespie, National Association of State Directors of Special Education; Marc Goldstein, American Physical Therapy Association; Candace Howes, Connecticut College; Richard Mainzer, Council for Exceptional Children; Laura Miller, National Association of Chain Drug Stores; Lisa Morris, University of South Maine; Patricia K. Ralabate, National Education Association; Paul R. Rao, National Rehabilitation Hospital; Dorie Seavey, Paraprofessional Healthcare Institute; and Robyn Stone, Institute for the Future of Aging Services, American Association of Homes and Services for the Aging.

Data collection, analysis, and writing for this book were originally conducted under a generous grant from the Alfred P. Sloan Foundation to Johns Hopkins University. A report to the Alfred P. Sloan Foundation titled Occupational Labor Shortages: Concepts, Causes, Consequences, and Cures was submitted in 2010. This original report to the Sloan Foundation has been revised and updated for this book. The authors would like to thank the Sloan Foundation for its generous grant, without which this book would not have been possible. The authors would also like to thank Brett Trutko for her work in updating analyses and revising and editing portions of the original manuscript prepared for the Sloan Foundation.

We would also like to thank those involved in the symposium cosponsored by the Economic Policy Institute (EPI), "Labor Shortages and Comprehensive Immigration Reform," which was held May 20, 2009, at EPI. Ross Eisenbrey of EPI worked with us to organize the symposium. Speakers included Philip Martin, University of California, Davis; Ron Hira, Rochester Institute of Technology; Norman Augustine, Lockheed Martin; Erling E. Boe, University of Pennsylvania; Phoebe Gillespie, National Association of State Directors of Special Education; Marc Goldstein, American Physical Therapy Association; Paul R. Rao, National Rehabilitation Hospital; Dale Belman, Michigan State University; Ray Marshall, University of Texas at Austin; Demetrios Papademetriou, Migration Policy Institute; Malcolm S. Cohen, Employment Research Corporation; Navjeet Singh, Commonwealth Corporation; Martin Ruhs, Migration Advisory Committee; Brian McCormick, FÁS; Karl Flecker, Canadian Labour Congress; Doris Meissner, Migration Policy Institute; Beryl

Howell, United States Sentencing Commission; Mark Regets, National Science Foundation; and Marc R. Rosenblum, Migration Policy Institute.

Finally, we would like to thank several individuals who provided additional information and comments. Kathleen Hyland of Civil Justice Inc. prepared part of the initial draft of the chapter on special education teachers. Karen Kosanovich of the Bureau of Labor Statistics assisted us by providing access to published and unpublished data. Brett Trutko of Deloitte LLP provided research assistance in updating the manuscript. Michael S. Teitelbaum of the Alfred P. Sloan Foundation provided valuable suggestions and guidance to the authors. We are grateful to all those who provided information and assistance. Any errors are the responsibility of the authors, not of those who so generously assisted us.

1
Conceptual Basis for Identifying and Measuring Occupational Labor Shortages

Three general issues regarding labor shortages have been widely discussed by economists and policymakers. First, because of recent declines in the U.S. birthrate, some analysts are concerned that there will simply be too few workers to maintain growth in the American economy (Levitan and Gallo 1989). Second, there has been a growing concern that there is or will be a serious mismatch between the skills of the American labor force and the needs of employers, resulting in a serious "skill gap" characterized by unfilled vacancies in many high-skill occupations along with high unemployment for less-skilled workers.[1] Finally, there has long been concern that shortages sometimes develop and persist in specific occupations, leading to inefficiencies in the U.S. economy. This third topic, occupation-specific shortages, is the primary subject of this study.

Before turning to the major topics of the chapter, it is instructive to consider why it is important to study occupational labor shortages. First, occupational labor shortages are of interest to educational and training institutions and their students because this information helps students choose fields of instruction where they are most likely to obtain jobs and where wage rates are likely to rise. Information on the tightness of various occupational labor markets is useful for counselors and students alike, enabling them to improve guidance and decision making. As discussed in Chapter 6, many states and local workforce investment areas are voting with their pocketbook to purchase "real-time labor market information" that provides detailed information on local labor market conditions for specific occupations.

At the national level, documenting current occupational labor shortages and projecting future shortages can help the nation identify and mitigate pipeline issues that impede the growth of some occupations. Are there enough training institutions in the country to eliminate current or projected shortages? Is the supply of instructors adequate to train sufficient entrants to the occupation?

Another national policy area where understanding shortages is important is the development of immigration and temporary foreign labor visa policies. Shortages in important occupations, such as physicians and nurses, may lead to situations where U.S. residents are denied critical services such as health care. On the other hand, if too many foreign workers are admitted, the domestic labor force may suffer unemployment or wage reductions.

Occupational labor shortages are more frequently found in labor markets that depart significantly from a free market with open entry and exit. Government interventions in such markets include directly or indirectly regulating wage rates, as is the case for public school teachers and many health care workers, and restricting supply through licensing. Understanding how shortages can arise in such an environment can be useful in establishing appropriate payment schemes for services. Two of the occupations analyzed here, home health workers and special education teachers, are subject to strong government roles in setting wage rates, so understanding how inappropriate policies can lead to shortages or less than the desired number or quality of workers in the occupation can be quite valuable.

Finally, the concept of an occupational labor shortage is, at first glance, puzzling to economists and others who have learned that the "invisible hand" of the marketplace described by Adam Smith should lead to markets clearing. It is this puzzle that first led us to study occupational shortages, and we have found that there are reasonable explanations for why shortages arise in occupations we have analyzed. Indeed, as we describe in the remainder of this chapter, there are a number of reasons consistent with conventional economic theory for why occupations can experience a shortage. In addition, we find situations that do not fit the economist's definition of a shortage but are problematic for the nation—the "social demand shortage" concept discussed later in this chapter.

In sum, labor markets do not always operate smoothly with supply and demand being equal at a given time. This book should help the reader understand why shortages arise, identify a shortage when present, and assess strategies to alleviate the shortage. As shown in the next section, many economists, including several U.S. Nobel Prize winners, have studied occupational shortages, and this volume builds on their work.

This chapter begins with an overview of the concept of occupational labor shortages, focusing on alternative definitions that have been used to identify occupation-specific labor shortages. This is followed by a discussion of the causes and consequences of occupational labor shortages.

BACKGROUND ON LABOR SHORTAGES

The term "labor shortage" has no universally agreed upon definition.[2] It sometimes refers to a shortfall in the total number of individuals in the labor force and sometimes denotes the possible mismatch between workers and jobs in the economy. Even when the term is used to refer to a particular occupation, several definitions have been proposed and used. In this report, the following definition of labor shortage is used: "A sustained market disequilibrium between supply and demand in which the quantity of workers demanded exceeds the supply available and willing to work at a particular wage and working conditions at a particular place and point in time."[3]

This definition considers a shortage as a disequilibrium condition where the amount of labor that workers are willing to supply is less than employers are willing to buy at the prevailing wage. A market is said to be in equilibrium when the amount of labor that workers (i.e., sellers) are willing to provide at the market price is equal to the amount that firms (i.e., purchasers) wish to buy at the market price. When the quantities that workers wish to provide and firms wish to buy are not identical at the prevailing price, the market is said to be in a disequilibrium situation.

If the quantity of labor offered exceeds the quantity that firms wish to purchase, there is a surplus, and if the quantity of labor desired by firms exceeds the amount workers offer at the prevailing price, there is a shortage. In general, the quantity that workers are willing to provide is an increasing function of the wages (i.e., price) they can obtain, and the relationship between wages and the amount that workers are willing to provide at various prices, with other factors held constant, is referred to as the labor supply curve.[4] Figure 1.1 shows a typical upward-sloping supply curve for labor. As the wage rate is increased, more workers are willing to enter a particular occupation and current workers are generally willing to provide more labor.

In Figure 1.1, the amount of labor that employers will wish to hire at alternative prices is indicated by the downward-sloping demand curve. Demand curves slope down because as the price of a factor increases, the employer will generally substitute other factors of production for the factor whose price has increased. In addition, higher factor prices will generally lead to higher product prices, which in turn will lead to a reduction in the quantity of the product demanded and in the factors of production.

The point labeled E in Figure 1.1 is the market equilibrium point. If the wage is equal to W_E, then the quantity of labor that workers are willing to supply at that wage (Q_E) is exactly equal to the quantity of labor that employers will wish to hire. The market is said to be in equilibrium because the quantity supplied is equal to the quantity demanded.

If, for some reason, the prevailing wage rate in the market is W_0 rather than W_E, then the quantity of labor that workers are willing to supply is equal to Q_S—the point on the supply curve corresponding to W_0. Employers, however, would like to hire Q_D at that wage rate. The difference between the amount of labor that employers wish to hire and the amount that workers are willing to provide ($Q_D - Q_S$) is the amount of the shortage. In the next section, we discuss how such shortages might arise.

Economists and other analysts have proposed several alternative definitions of occupational shortages.[5] Although these definitions are generally not used in this report, it is important to note that others use the term differently. It is particularly important to keep the definition in mind when interpreting other studies of shortages.

The Social Demand Model

Some analysts consider a shortage to be present if the number of workers in an occupation is fewer than what is considered the socially desired number. Under this definition, a shortage of engineers exists if the analyst making the determination concludes that society would be

Figure 1.1 Illustration of a Labor Shortage

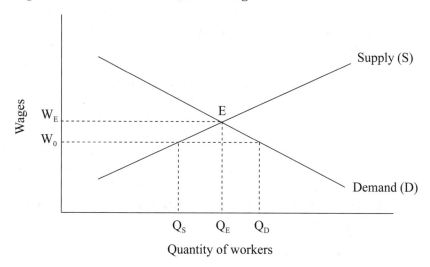

better off if there were more engineers. This type of definition does not imply that the labor market is in disequilibrium; instead it describes a situation where the person who claims there is a shortage does not like the market's results. Arrow and Capron (1959) explain the problem with this definition as follows:

> In particular, careful reading of such statements indicates that the speakers have in effect been saying: There are not as many engineers and scientists as this nation should have in order to do all the things that need doing such as maintaining our rapid rate of technological progress, raising our standard of living, keeping us militarily strong, etc. In other words, they are saying that (in the economic sense) demand for technically skilled manpower ought to be greater than it is—it is really a shortage of demand for scientists and engineers that concerns them. (p. 307)

For example, in the late 1980s, the Secretary of Health and Human Services' Commission on Nursing stated in an assessment of labor market conditions for registered nurses that "in the most general terms, a registered nurse [RN] shortage exists when the supply of RNs is insufficient to meet the 'requirements' for RNs. RN requirements can be defined based on either economic demand or clinical need" (U.S. Department of Health and Human Services [DHHS] 1988, p. 3). The

Commission rejected the use of clinical need for defining a shortage because it concluded that there is no objective method of quantifying the degree of the shortage and relating it to specific factors.

The fact that we do not use this type of definition for a shortage does not mean we believe that it is unimportant for the nation to consider whether it is satisfied with market-produced results. Quite the contrary, it is important for society to consider whether or not the market solutions are desirable and, if not, to take appropriate actions. One concern in this volume is with the operation of labor markets and the reasons why labor markets sometimes fail to achieve equilibrium, and actions that can be taken to improve their efficiency; however, in some of the occupations examined, there is evidence of a potential social demand shortage, and we identify the potential problems even if an economic type of shortage does not exist.

The Blank-Stigler Model

One of the first major studies of occupational shortages was conducted by David S. Blank and George J. Stigler (1957). Blank and Stigler define a shortage as follows: "A shortage exists when the number of workers available (the supply) increases less rapidly than the number demanded *at the salaries paid in the recent past*" (p. 24). Blank and Stigler then argue that to alleviate the shortage, wages in the occupation must rise, and some of the work formerly performed by the occupation with the shortage will now be performed by others.

The Blank-Stigler shortage concept is illustrated in Figure 1.2. Initially the market is in equilibrium at E with wage rate W_E and Q_E workers. If demand increases, the demand curve will shift to the right to line D_1. A shortage will result if the wage remains at W_E because employers will wish to hire Q_1 workers—but only Q_E workers will be available at that wage. Market pressures will then lead to an increase in the wage, and equilibrium will eventually be restored with a new wage of W_2 and with Q_2 workers.

There are several problems with the Blank-Stigler model. First, as discussed below, an increase in demand is only one possible cause of a shortage. Thus, the Blank-Stigler model ignores other possible causes of occupational shortages. Second, Blank and Stigler indicate that a shortage can be identified by rising wages in the affected occupation.

Figure 1.2 Illustration of Blank-Stigler and Arrow-Capron Shortages

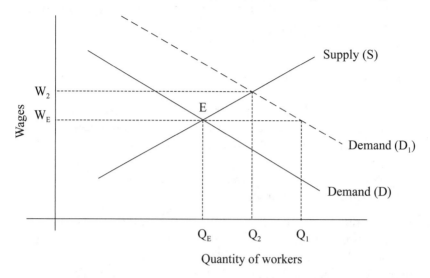

Wages may not rise, however, because of market imperfections such as wage controls or imperfect information.

The Arrow-Capron Dynamic Shortage Model

Arrow and Capron (1959) developed an alternative model of occupational shortages. Their definition, which they refer to as a dynamic shortage, is based on the premise that "a steady upward shift in the demand curve over a period of time will produce a shortage, that is, a situation in which there are unfilled vacancies in positions where salaries are the same as those currently being paid in others of the same type and quality" (p. 301).

The Arrow-Capron model is also illustrated in Figure 1.2. Like the Blank-Stigler model, the Arrow-Capron model is characterized by increased demand. However, Arrow and Capron note that markets are characterized by a "reaction speed," and that institutional arrangements (such as long-term contracts) and the time it takes for information to spread will affect the time required for employers to adjust wages. Thus, Arrow and Capron conclude that shortages will be characterized by vacancies. In Figure 1.2, the number of vacancies initially resulting from the increase in demand will be equal to $Q_1 - Q_E$. If demand continues to grow, then the market may not achieve equilibrium. The Arrow-Capron dynamic shortage model is consistent with the general model used here, but it may be considered a specific case.

Other Definitions of Shortages

In addition to the definitions presented above, several other definitions for shortages have been proposed. Harrington and Sum (1984) review several other possible definitions of occupational labor shortages, and two of them are briefly discussed below.

The rate of return model

The "rate of return model" is based on the application of internal rate of return analysis to alternative occupations. The costs of investing in a particular occupation are defined as the sum of the direct costs for higher education, training, and supplies, plus the indirect costs of foregone wages that are incurred during periods of training. The benefits are the earnings typically derived from the occupation each year. The internal rate of return is then calculated by finding the interest rate that equates the present value of the costs and benefits.[6] Occupations with shortages are thus defined as those occupations with higher than average rates of return.

Harrington and Sum note that the rate of return approach is "beset with numerous methodological and measurement difficulties." One important problem is that we cannot observe future earnings streams from various occupations. Relying on cross-sectional or historical data may provide a misleading picture of what the earnings will eventually be. In addition, the returns on various occupations may differ for reasons having little to do with a shortage. For example, some occupations may pay higher wages because they have high health or safety risks—what economists refer to as compensating differentials.

The monopsonistic labor model

A market where there is only one buyer for a particular good or type of labor is referred to as a monopsony. The monopsonist differs from an employer in a competitive labor market because the monopsonist can set the wage rather than act as a price taker. The situation for a monopsonist is illustrated in Figure 1.3. Because the monopsonist is the only buyer for the occupation of interest, the monopsonist observes the labor supply curve for the occupation; this is in contrast to an employer in a competitive market who can hire all the labor desired at the market wage. Because the monopsonistic employer must pay all workers the same wage, the monopsonist faces a steep upward sloping marginal labor cost curve—if an additional worker is hired, wages must be increased for all currently employed workers as well as the marginal worker. Figure 1.3 also illustrates the marginal revenue product curve for the firm. To maximize profits, the monopsonist employer will hire labor until the marginal labor cost is equal to the marginal revenue product, corresponding to the point X in the figure. The wage paid by the monopsonist will then be W_M, and Q_M workers will be hired. Note that the number of workers hired is fewer than in a competitive market (Q_E), and the wage is lower than the competitive wage (W_E).

The monopsonist might consider the resulting situation to be a shortage because the monopsonist would like to hire more workers at the monopsony wage. However, because the monopsonist faces an upward

Figure 1.3 Illustration of Labor Demand by a Monopsonist

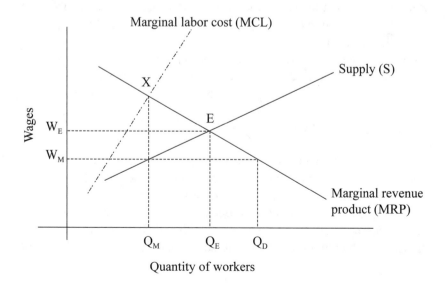

Quantity of workers

sloping labor supply curve, the wage must be increased to attract additional labor into the occupation. Ehrenberg and Smith (2009) conclude that the labor shortage faced by a monopsonist is "more apparent than real" because the monopsonist is hiring the quantity of labor desired at the wage offered. In addition, Ehrenberg and Smith point out that monopsony situations are probably very rare.

Concepts from Butz et al.

Butz et al. (2003) describe five possible meanings of an occupational shortage:

1) if production is lower than in the recent past;

2) if competitors' share of total production is growing;

3) if production is lower than what the people doing the producing would like;

4) if less is produced than the nation is deemed to need; and

5) if production is not meeting market demand, as indicated by a rising price.

Although all of these concepts may signify a problem from some perspective, only the final definition corresponds to the economic concept of an occupational shortage. Although the first three concepts listed by Butz et al. may well be cause for concern for a firm, they are more indicative of a shortfall in desired production than any type of occupational shortage. The fourth concept, producing less than the nation is deemed to need, corresponds to the social demand concept of a shortage introduced by Arrow and Capron (1959).

Summary of Shortage Concepts

Some of the labor shortage concepts that have been proposed, such as looking at the total amount of labor supplied and the potential economy-wide mismatch between employer needs and worker qualifications, are important, but they are not relevant to the study of occupational shortages. As the Secretary of Health and Human Services' Commission on Nursing concluded, the social demand concept is difficult to apply because there is no objective way of determining the optimal number of workers in various professions.

Definitions proposed in the 1950s by Blank and Stigler (1957) and by Arrow and Capron (1959) are closer to the concept of a labor shortage that is used here. The principal advantage of these definitions is that they provide relatively straightforward tests for the existence of a shortage—rising relative wages in the case of the Blank-Stigler definition and increasing vacancies in the case of the Arrow-Capron definition. However, these definitions are too narrow to capture all the types of shortages of interest. Both the Blank-Stigler and Arrow-Capron definitions do not include labor market situations classified as shortages by the other definition, and both omit situations where excess demand results from market imperfections. The more general definition employed here covers such cases.

The use of a broad definition does have some disadvantages. As Franke and Sobel (1970) note in using a similar definition, "The definition is neither altogether concrete and precise nor is it susceptible to precise measurements." However, we also concur with Franke and Sobel's conclusion that "viewed in the context of a study whose purpose is to examine the degree to which labor market institutions respond to and facilitate adjustment to varying degrees of labor market tightness, the definition is, however, meaningful and operational" (p. 7).

CAUSES OF LABOR SHORTAGES

There are several reasons why it is important to address the causes and consequences of labor shortages. First, because we have adopted a fairly broad definition of a shortage, we will have no single indicator that a shortage exists. By reviewing the economic theory of the causes and consequences of shortages, we will be aware of the appropriate market signals to look for in assessing whether or not a shortage exists. This is especially important because under certain conditions, various interest groups have incentives to argue that a shortage is present or absent. For example, employers and trade associations sometimes have an incentive to claim that there is a shortage to increase immigration quotas for particular occupations, giving them access to a broader pool of applicants. At other times, employers might find it in their interest to claim there are no shortages, in order to gain better leverage in contract negotiations with their workforce.

Another important reason for analyzing the causes and consequences of shortages is to help identify and assess potential public and private policies for dealing with shortages. Being able to identify causes will help interested parties focus on the relevant developments in labor and product markets. Understanding the consequences will help us to assess what interventions, if any, are appropriate by government, employers, and workers.

Before turning to the causes and consequences of labor shortages, it is useful to note some of the dimensions of shortages:

- **Geographic scope of the shortage**. Depending on the occupation and the nature of the market, labor markets can be national or regional in scope. Similarly, a particular occupation may have a nationwide shortage, or the shortage may be confined to a few labor markets or a single region of the country (e.g., the shipyard industry on the Gulf Coast).

- **Longevity of the shortage**. As will be discussed below, various forces act to bring markets into and out of equilibrium. Thus, shortages can be relatively brief, lasting for a few weeks or months, or prolonged, lasting for one or more years.

- **Severity of the shortage**. Unlike the two dimensions discussed above, it is not easy to develop good measures of the severity of a shortage. Conceptually, we can measure the severity of a shortage in terms of the magnitude of the changes in wages required to restore equilibrium or in terms of the number of workers needed to alleviate the shortage. There are several difficulties with these concepts. First, we do not generally observe the supply and demand curves for specific occupations. Thus, we cannot directly estimate the size of the employment or wage gap of a shortage. Second, even if we could measure supply and demand, it would not be easy to classify a particular gap as large or small, especially when comparing across occupations—occupations vary significantly in their normal vacancy rates and wage dispersion. Thus, a high vacancy rate for one occupation with a shortage may be characteristic of another occupation in equilibrium.

- **Subspecialty shortages**. Up to this point we have considered occupations as if they are uniform. For some occupations this may be correct, but for others there may be differentiation by subspecialty (e.g., emergency room nurses), years of work experience, or specialized training. In such cases, a shortage may exist for the entire occupation or only for workers with selected characteristics. For example, training for engineers has changed considerably over the past 20 years, and older electrical engineers may not be good substitutes for new engineers who have more training in designing integrated circuits. Likewise, new tool and die makers may not be good substitutes for experienced tool and die makers who have gained additional skills through their work. The key determinant of whether there can be shortages for some parts of an occupation is whether all workers within the occupation are reasonable substitutes for each other. If not, a shortage can exist within an occupation while other subcategories are in equilibrium or even in surplus. As will be shown below, subspecialty shortages can be difficult to document because labor market trends are only captured at a broader level. For example, the Standard Occupational Classification (SOC) system in the United States considers all computer programmers to be in a single occupation. However, when employers have an opening, it will be for a programmer who can write code in a particular language, such as HTML, and a COBOL programmer would not meet those needs. Thus, looking at data for all types of programmers combined could mask the presence of a shortage of a particular type of programmer.

For an occupation to have a shortage, two conditions are necessary. First, the occupation must be in disequilibrium, where the number of workers employers wish to hire exceeds the number willing to work at the prevailing wage. Second, the market must adjust slowly, if at all, with the achievement of equilibrium requiring a substantial period of time. We first discuss the reasons why markets are sometimes in disequilibrium. We then examine the adjustments that employers make to alleviate the disequilibrium, followed by a discussion of the reasons why disequilibria may persist. We then discuss the consequences of prolonged shortages.

REASONS WHY OCCUPATIONAL LABOR MARKETS ARE IN DISEQUILIBRIUM

Labor shortages can result from a number of different causes. In this section, we discuss the reasons why the labor market for a particular occupation might leave an equilibrium situation where the market wage equates supply and demand.[7]

Increase in the Demand for Labor

Figure 1.4 illustrates how a labor shortage can result from an increase in the demand for labor; several variants of this scenario were discussed previously. Suppose that the labor market is initially in equilibrium at point E. If the demand for labor increases, the demand curve will shift to the right. If the supply curve remains the same and the prevailing price (wage) remains at W_E, employers would like to hire Q_D workers, but only Q_E will be available. Thus, there will be a shortage of $Q_D - Q_E$ workers.

The demand for labor by employers can increase for several reasons. Perhaps the most likely reason for an increase in the demand for labor is an increase in the demand for the goods or services produced by employers (e.g., a substantial expansion in contracts to shipyards for construction and/or repair of ships). An increase in the demand for the product can result from an increase in the number of consumers, an increase in the income or wealth of consumers, a change in the composition of the population of buyers, or changes in the tastes of consumers.

Another potential reason for an increase in the demand for labor is an increase in the prices of substitute factors of production. For example, in a hospital the demand for nurses might increase if the wage rates of doctors or nurse's aides increases. The demand for a given type of labor will also increase if the price of a nonlabor factor (e.g., raw materials or machinery) increases and the labor can be used as a substitute

Figure 1.4 Illustration of a Labor Shortage Arising from an Increase in Labor Demand

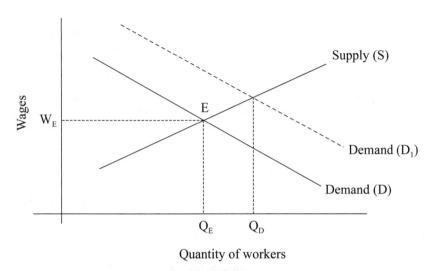

Quantity of workers

in the production process. Both the Arrow-Capron and Blank-Stigler labor shortage models discussed previously are demand-driven shortage models. The Arrow-Capron dynamic model is somewhat more complex because it deals with a situation where demand continually grows more rapidly than supply.

An increase in demand for labor in a particular occupation does not necessarily lead to a shortage. If the supply of labor to an occupation can respond to the increased demand, the result will be a new equilibrium with more workers employed and a higher wage rate than at the previous equilibrium, as is illustrated in Figure 1.4. An increase in demand will almost certainly require some time for the market to reach a new equilibrium, but if vacancies persist for a sustained period, the occupation can be characterized as experiencing a shortage. Reasons why occupational labor markets may adjust slowly are discussed below.

Decrease in the Supply of Labor

A decrease in the supply of labor to a particular market can also create a labor shortage. This situation is illustrated in Figure 1.5. Once again suppose that the market is originally in equilibrium at point E. If

**Figure 1.5 Illustration of a Labor Shortage Arising from a Decrease in
Labor Supply**

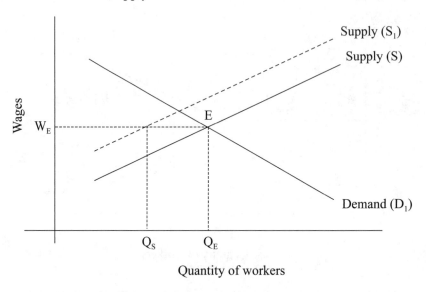

the labor supply curve is shifted to the left, indicating fewer workers
available at each wage rate, there will be a labor shortage if the prevailing wage remains at W_E. Employers will still be trying to hire Q_E workers, but only Q_S workers will be available after the supply decreases.
Thus, there will be a shortage of $Q_E - Q_S$ workers.

The labor supply curve for the labor market in question might shift
for several reasons. One potential cause is a decrease in the size of the
population that works in the relevant jobs. For example, as the baby-
boom generation has aged, employers who generally hire young people as they complete high school have suddenly faced a much smaller
supply of entry-level workers from the so-called baby-bust generation,
which has a much smaller population.

The supply curve might also shift to the left because wages in other
occupations have risen, making employment in the market of interest less attractive, or because nonwork opportunities, such as welfare,
crime, and retirement, have become more attractive.[8] Finally, the labor
supply curve for an occupation might shift to the left because of restrictions on entry into the relevant labor market. Such restrictions may be

implemented by the government (through licensing requirements and restrictions on the number of licenses granted), professional organizations that set standards for practice, labor unions, or training institutions (e.g., universities or community colleges).

Restrictions on Prices

Although most prices are determined competitively by markets in the United States, the price of labor or the price of the final product is regulated in some industries. For example, cities generally regulate the price that taxi drivers can charge. In such instances, the supply curve is truncated at the regulated price. This situation is illustrated in Figure 1.6. The wage rate is restricted to be no higher than W_M, so the supply curve at higher wages is indicated by a dashed line. The labor that will be supplied at that wage is Q_S. At that wage, however, the demand is for Q_D workers, so there is a shortage of $Q_D - Q_S$ workers. An example of this type of shortage during some periods is the U.S. government's market for entry-level PhD economists. The federal government traditionally hires entry-level economists at the GS-12 pay level, and agencies

Figure 1.6 Illustration of Labor Shortage Arising from Restrictions on Wages

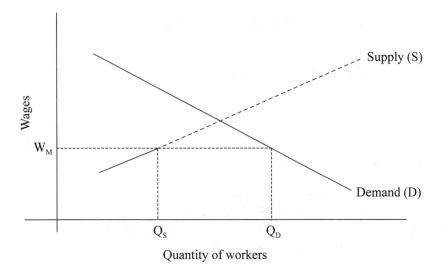

are generally not permitted to pay a higher wage rate. Sometimes the market wage for entry-level economists is higher, so there is sometimes a shortage of entry-level PhD economists in government agencies.

More commonly, the government regulates the prices of products and services rather than labor. In industries where labor comprises a relatively small share of the product's price, such as in the generation of electric power, the product price regulation is not likely to cause a labor shortage. In very labor-intensive industries, however, output price regulation can be tantamount to regulating the price of labor. Examples include the health care industry in general and the home care industry in particular. A large share of the U.S. health industry is financed by the Medicare and Medicaid programs. In the case of Medicare, the federal government limits the reimbursements that providers can obtain for treating covered elderly patients. State governments provide similar regulation under Medicaid programs for the poor. Because the government restricts the charges that providers can make, the providers face limits on what they can pay workers and still cover their costs.

ADJUSTMENTS TO OCCUPATIONAL SHORTAGES BY EMPLOYERS

This section describes some of the actions that firms are likely to take to deal with labor imbalances. Employers will first note problems when they are unable to fill vacancies at current wage rates, and they will therefore likely take actions to deal with the unfilled positions. Some actions are less costly and more reversible than others, so employers are likely to undertake these actions first. The potential actions that employers can take are listed roughly in order of desirability from the employer's point of view. In particular cases, of course, some of the potential actions may be inapplicable or employers may undertake the actions in a different order. Note that all the potential actions employers can take are the opposite of the actions that lead to vacancies: increasing supply, decreasing demand, and increasing wages. Finally, many of the actions described below may be undertaken by employers for reasons other than trying to fill vacant positions.

Increase Recruiting Efforts

A logical first step to fill vacancies is to increase recruiting efforts. Although employers will incur short-term costs in expanding recruiting, there are no long-term or permanent costs involved. Recruiting can be increased through several approaches:

- **Increase advertising in the usual outlets.** For example, employers who advertise in newspapers can increase the frequency of the advertisements or the size of the advertisements to attract more attention to vacancies.

- **Advertise in other media.** To reach a wider audience of potential employees, firms can expand their advertising campaigns. Firms that traditionally recruit through newspaper advertisements can add other newspapers in the community or increase the use of radio and television advertising. Use of job fairs is another such technique. Over the past decade, employers have increasingly advertised available positions over the Internet, using the company's Web site, trade association Web sites, and other more generalized job search Web sites (e.g., Monster .com, CareerBuilder.com, and CareerLink.com).

- **Expand the recruiting area.** Employers who believe that the problem is local rather than regional or national can increase the geographical scope of their recruiting efforts. For example, a firm having difficulty recruiting shipfitters in Louisiana might expand its recruiting efforts to other nearby areas along the Gulf Coast (e.g., Texas, Mississippi, and Florida) and, if necessary, in other parts of the country or world. Some occupations, generally those with highly skilled jobs, already have national labor markets. For these firms, and for firms recruiting for occupations with a national shortage, the only way to increase the recruiting market is to recruit abroad. The extreme case of expanding the recruiting area is to recruit immigrants either for temporary or permanent jobs. Because the number and characteristics of immigrants that can be admitted is determined by law, individual employers may be limited in the extent to which they can make use of this option.

- **Use public and private employment agencies**. Firms that do not already do so can make use of public and private employment agencies. Public agencies, referred to as the employment service or job service, are free to both workers and employers. In some states, the employment service may tend to specialize in serving particular types of workers, but all employers can list their openings with the employment service. Private employment agencies charge a fee to either the worker or the firm, with the fee based either on the time spent by the agency or as a percentage of the hired worker's salary.

- **Pay recruiting bonuses to employees who bring in new workers**. For many employers, current workers are often the best source of potential new hires. Employees are likely to be hesitant to recommend individuals who are unqualified, and the candidates they recommend are likely to know more about the work and working conditions than other job candidates. Thus, for many firms, current employees are a major source of job applicants. To encourage workers to assist in the recruiting process, employers sometimes offer a bonus for referring qualified applicants or applicants who are hired.

Increase Use of Overtime

A relatively simple solution to the problem of filling vacancies is to have current employees work more hours. Employers who anticipate that the problem will not last for a substantial period of time are likely to use this approach. If the workers are exempt from the overtime provisions of the Fair Labor Standards Act (FLSA) and do not receive a premium for hours in excess of 40 hours per week, overtime may actually save money relative to hiring additional workers. Even for nonexempt workers, overtime may be less expensive because many fringe benefits (such as health insurance, unemployment insurance, and workers compensation) are fixed per worker, and the firm will not experience any increase in costs for these benefits when current employees work additional hours, and other costs (such as recruitment and training) can be avoided.

As a long-term measure, however, increased use of overtime may not be a viable option. For workers not exempt from the FLSA, the employer must pay a premium of at least 50 percent for overtime work, which gives employers a strong financial incentive to try other means to deal with vacancy problems. In addition, many workers prefer not to work overtime, so increased use of overtime may lead to employee dissatisfaction and increased turnover, thereby exacerbating the vacancy problem instead of reducing it.

Reduce Minimum Qualifications for the Job

Another method of filling vacancies is to reduce the minimum hiring standards for the occupation. At first this may appear damaging, but this is not necessarily the case. The firm may have set the minimum hiring qualifications higher than necessary when labor was abundant. For example, a firm may have required a college degree for sales workers when a high school diploma would have been adequate. For professional jobs, the firm may have selected graduates from the most prestigious schools, or have had a minimum grade point average or test score cutoff, and these requirements may not be necessary.

If the productivity of less qualified workers is lower, the firm may be able to train the workers to reach the productivity levels of the more qualified workers after a reasonable period of time. When a firm reduces the minimum hiring qualifications, the labor supply is effectively increased, and the firm may be able to reduce the wages offered or at least avoid increasing wages.

Restructure Work to Use Current or New Employees in Other Occupations

If employers have difficulty filling vacancies with workers in one occupation, it is sometimes possible to restructure the work to make use of workers in other occupations. For example, hospital services are performed by workers in a number of occupations, such as physicians, nurses, nurse's aides, and orderlies. Although some duties cannot be readily reassigned (only physicians can perform major surgery), nurses can perform some of the testing, and care-taking functions can be assumed by virtually any of the staff. Likewise, some engineering tasks can be performed by drafters, and some tasks performed by teachers can be handled by aides.

For several reasons, firms will not always make use of this option. Although it is often possible to reassign some tasks from higher-skilled to lower-skilled workers, it is seldom possible to go in the other direction. For example, hospitals are unlikely to use physicians to perform care-taking tasks because physicians are so costly that other measures will generally be less expensive. In addition, assigning what is perceived to be low-level work to employees may hurt morale and productivity. Finally, reassigning tasks may involve considerable expense and disruption because of training and rescheduling that must be conducted.

In some cases, complex jobs can be decomposed into simpler tasks that can be handled by less-skilled workers. For example, a tool and die maker's work could be split among metal workers who possess some, but not all, of the skills of a tool and die maker. In general, shortages are more likely to occur for high-skill occupations than low-skill occupations.

Substitute Machinery and Equipment for Labor

Employers can sometimes alter the production process to replace workers with equipment. As technology has advanced in recent years, the types of tasks performed by machines have also changed. Formerly, machines typically replaced humans in unskilled tasks such as lifting and moving. More recently, computer-based technology permits machines to perform more sophisticated tasks, including voice recognition, drawing, designing, and (to some extent) teaching. Artificial intelligence "expert system" models even permit computers to substitute for professional judgment under certain circumstances.

There are obviously limits to how much technology can substitute for labor, and in many situations technology will be used to substitute for labor for reasons other than difficulty in filling job openings. However, substituting technology for labor is sometimes a viable method of dealing with difficulty in filling vacancies.

Train Workers for the Jobs

For some occupations, training is traditionally performed by employers, either formally through apprenticeship or other training programs or informally through on-the-job training. For many other occupations, however, training for entry-level jobs is performed by other means—typically colleges and universities for professional occupations, and vocational schools and trade schools for skilled craft and service occupations. Employers who traditionally do not train their own workers may resort to offering or sponsoring training if they are experiencing difficulty in filling vacancies.

Offering training for an occupation is often a major commitment for employers, and it is typically not provided unless most other approaches fail. There are several related reasons why firms are reluctant to offer occupational training. First, training is generally time-consuming. Training new employees for a skilled occupation can sometimes take years, and by the time the workers are trained, the problem of filling vacancies may have disappeared. Second, establishing and operating a training program to bring new employees into an occupation is costly. Employers must feel confident that they can recoup their investment before they are willing to underwrite these costs. Finally, training new hires for occupations with vacancies carries several risks for employers. The individuals selected may not be able to successfully complete the training, or if the skills are transferable to other employers, they may quit shortly after they are trained.[9]

For occupations that do not require a college degree, establishing an apprenticeship program is one potential method of training workers for occupations through a combination of classroom and on-the-job training. Other possibilities include training current or new workers in-house or in cooperation with local colleges, vocational schools, and proprietary schools. In some cases the employer may not pay for the training—the courses can be partially or fully funded under federal programs such as the Workforce Investment Act (WIA), state training programs, or educational institutions.

Training for entry into an occupation can be illustrated by an extreme but interesting case. The uniformed services need physicians, but they are prohibited from paying market wages to physicians (a shortage induced by market restrictions). To get around this problem, the uniformed services established their own medical school, Uniformed Services University, to train physicians at no cost to the students. To prevent the students from leaving soon after being trained, the students are required to sign contracts agreeing to stay in the military for a specified number of years.

Improve Working Conditions

Improving working conditions sometimes is an effective way to attract new workers and/or reduce turnover. Working conditions include factors such as hours worked, upgrades in equipment and facilities used by workers, level and type of supervision, involvement in operation of the firm, training to deal with stress related to the job, and recognition of the importance of workers in the occupation. Improvements in working conditions can be especially useful in situations where vacancies are created by high turnover. High turnover is often associated with occupations that have high stress, low wages, or low prestige. A concomitant benefit of improving working conditions is that productivity may increase as well.

Improving the number or timing of work hours can also help in recruiting new workers and in reducing vacancies. Some occupations may require split shifts (e.g., driving buses), night and weekend work (e.g., health occupations), or down time between productive periods (e.g., home care). Employers sometimes deal with these unpleasant working conditions by offering premiums for work at undesirable times, but they often believe they cannot afford a sufficiently high shift differential to eliminate the problem. Although shift differentials are still often necessary for undesirable shifts, employers can sometimes improve recruiting and reduce turnover by working with employees to structure shifts to be as desirable as feasible. For example, hospitals have experimented with a number of shift structures to fill the most undesirable shifts. In the home care industry, where workers sometimes have a great deal of travel time and down time between cases, some employers have been successful in restructuring caseloads to minimize these problems.

Offer Bonuses to New Employees

Although this approach is not commonly used, firms sometimes offer new employees bonuses for joining the firm. Signing bonuses are similar to paying current employees bonuses (or "bounties") for recruiting new employees for occupations that are difficult to fill, except that bonuses go to the new employees rather than the current employees.

For workers, this option provides an extra incentive to join the firm offering the bonuses. This approach is more advantageous for employers than raising wages because it is a one-time cost and only affects the employees added in the occupation of interest. The disadvantage for employers is that the employees lured by such bonuses may not be as interested in long-term careers with the firm, and they may be "pirated" away by other firms offering similar bonuses. Signing bonuses are most frequently used when employers feel that they are under intense pressure to fill vacancies in the short run. When employers recognize this to be the case, they sometimes resort to using hiring bonuses to lure employees from other firms. Hiring bonuses have been used by hospitals to recruit nurses and by data processing firms to recruit programmers.

Improve Wages and Fringe Benefits

Based on the simple supply and demand curve analysis, increasing wages is an obvious way to increase the number of workers willing to work in a particular occupation. Employers are generally reluctant to increase wages for several reasons. First, an increase in wages will affect the entire workforce in the occupation with vacancies, not just the new workers the firm wishes to attract. Thus, the employer incurs costs for more than just the added workers.

Second, the employer might have to increase wages for workers in other occupations as well. Employers generally attempt to maintain equity among workers in various occupations. Thus, if an employer increases wages for one occupation because of difficulties in filling vacancies, wages may have to be increased for other occupations as well to maintain what are viewed as appropriate differentials. Another problem with raising wages is that wages tend to be "sticky" in terms of moving down. That is, once market conditions change, employers will generally have less flexibility to reduce wages later. Finally, raising wages might not be an effective means of recruiting in the short run if supply is not responsive to changes in wages (i.e., the supply is inelastic). In the extreme case, if the supply is totally fixed in the short run, higher wages cannot induce any change in the number of workers qualified to work in the occupation.

Improving fringe benefits is similar to increasing wages, but in some instances employers will reduce their vacancy rates more by improving benefits rather than by increasing wages by a similar amount. For example, health insurance is often an important fringe benefit to provide. Because group health insurance rates are usually substantially less expensive than individual policies, the value of health insurance to the employee will often be greater than the cost to the employer. Health insurance is especially a concern for employers trying to fill vacancies for relatively low-paying jobs if Temporary Assistance for Needy Families (TANF) recipients are potential workers.[10] This is because TANF recipients receive health insurance through the Medicaid program, and they are often hesitant to take jobs if they will lose coverage for themselves and their children. Unfortunately, many employers who do not provide health insurance are small and pay low wages. Thus, adding benefits such as health insurance may be most burdensome in those cases where it would be most important. Other potential fringe benefits include subsidized housing and child care.

Contract Out the Work

If a firm is unable to hire all the employees it needs in particular occupations, the firm may be able to contract out the work to another employer who is not experiencing shortages. In some instances, the labor problem may be regional in nature, and the firm can contract out the work to a firm in another part of the country. If the problem is nationwide, the firm can sometimes have the work performed overseas.

Turn Down Work

If a firm has exhausted all means that it considers reasonable and can find no reasonable way around its occupational vacancies, the firm always has the option of turning down work. Employers generally use this "solution" only as a last resort because they do not like to give up customers to competitors, and, more basically, the only way to make a profit is to sell goods and services.

If the firm has limited capacity to conduct its business because of occupational shortages, there are more subtle measures than simply refusing work. For example, the firm might reduce its marketing activity, thereby reducing the demand for its products as well as its advertising costs.

REASONS LABOR MARKETS MAY ADJUST SLOWLY

As discussed above, labor markets, and other markets as well, constantly experience changes in supply and demand that cause them to deviate from an equilibrium situation. In most cases, firms and workers will take actions that will move the labor market toward equilibrium. In some instances, however, the market adjusts slowly, and equilibrium is not restored, resulting in a shortage for the occupation. The literature suggests several factors that may result in the market failing to clear reasonably quickly. These factors are discussed below.

Slow Reaction Time by Employers

In most industries, each individual firm employs a small share of the workers in a particular occupation. Thus, individual employers may be unaware of an increase in demand, and they are almost certainly unaware of the magnitude of the increase. As the firm recognizes that workers cannot be attracted at what they believe to be the market wage, they may then take the actions described above to deal with the vacancies.

A number of factors can influence the reaction time of employers. If the firm does not recruit frequently for the occupation, either because of low turnover or because it employs few workers in the occupation, the firm may not know the typical period for filling vacancies for that occupation. The firm also may not have a good idea of what the market wage is and may tend to set its offer wage too low.

Several institutional factors are likely to affect reaction time by employers. Occupations characterized by long vacancy periods are more likely to have slow reaction times by employers because employers expect to take a significant amount of time before they fill vacancies. Lengthy recruiting periods are more characteristic of occupations with high salaries, typically professional and managerial occupations and highly skilled craft jobs. Occupations where employment is concentrated in small firms are likely to be characterized by slow reaction times because the employers are likely to recruit for fewer positions and less frequently than larger employers.

Other institutional factors that can influence employer reaction time include the extent to which employers and workers in the occupation are organized and exchange information. For example, if employers have a trade association that monitors and publishes data on wages, vacancies, and other employment-related factors, employers will be aware of the occupational situation early in the search process. Of course, receiving national-level data is not as useful as local data for an employer who recruits locally. For some occupations, hiring is done in conjunction with the trade union representing the workers. Even if most firms are small, the centralization of the hiring process will help employers gain a quicker grasp of the supply available.

Slow Response Time by Employers

After firms recognize that there is excess demand for an occupation, they may delay taking actions to fill their vacancies. Most strategies that a firm might try could be risky, expensive, or both. Relatively minor responses, such as intensifying the recruiting effort, will waste the firm's money if the positions would be filled without them. More significant responses, such as changing the occupational structure of the firm and training workers, require major commitments of time and resources to plan and implement. Such actions are unlikely to be taken unless the employer believes that the firm is facing a prolonged period of difficulty in hiring.

Increasing wages can also be a major step for employers. As noted above, the wage increases must also be passed on to current workers as well as the newly hired workers, and sometimes workers in other occupations must receive increases as well. If the firm is in a competitive product market, it must carefully balance two competing interests. If it sets the wage too high, the firm's costs will be higher than the costs of its competitors, and the firm is likely to either lose market share (if it passes the costs on to consumers) or profits (if it absorbs the increased costs) or both. Thus, firms are likely to be conservative in increasing wages as a method of filling vacancies.

Slow Reaction Time by Workers

Workers in other occupations and individuals who are unemployed or out of the labor force may not immediately recognize that wages or working conditions have improved in the occupation with the developing shortage. If workers who might be attracted to jobs in the occupation with the excess demand are unaware of the opportunities, they will not be able to consider entering that occupation. The time required for workers to become aware of the new opportunities depends on how effective firms' recruiting strategies are and how sensitive workers are to the recruiting effort. Also, workers may have a certain amount of loyalty to their current employer, occupation, or industry, and the greater such loyalty is, the slower the reaction time by workers.

Slow Response Time by Workers

Once workers are aware of the opportunities, their response time will depend on the time required to qualify for the positions and the costs and benefits of obtaining any needed qualifications, applying for the positions, and changing jobs. Typically, the greater the incentives provided by employers to induce workers into the occupation of interest, the quicker and greater the response by potential entrants.

For many occupations, training time is the most important factor slowing worker response time. Occupations requiring a specialized college degree, such as engineering, will be very slow in adjusting because the "pipeline" for producing new engineers is four years. The lag might be more extensive if some potential engineers must adjust their mathematics course load in high school. Some specialized occupations, such as architecture and medicine, require even longer preparation.

Many occupations requiring less than a college education still demand several years of training and will have a substantial lag before interested individuals qualify for the occupation. For example, many technician and skilled craft positions require two or more years of training. At the other extreme, some low-skill jobs, including paraprofessional home health care workers, may require as little as one week of formal training. Thus, the worker response lag generally will be shorter.

Response time can also be slowed if training institutions lack the capacity to train additional workers. For instance, the supply of nurses cannot be readily expanded if there are too few nursing instructors.

Restrictions on Occupational Entry

In some cases, institutional barriers to occupational entry will slow down the adjustment process. These restrictions are generally instituted to achieve certain purposes, so removing or modifying the barriers is not always appropriate. However, in times of occupational shortages, consideration is often given to modifying these restrictions.

One example of a barrier to occupational entry is limits in the enrollment capacity of training institutions that supply workers for the occupation. Suppose, for instance, that hospitals needed to hire more physicians and there were enough individuals interested in attending medical school to meet the hospitals' demands. If the nation's medical schools could not admit the extra students because of limited capacity, the supply of physicians could not increase. Note that hospitals do not regulate the capacity of medical schools, so it would be difficult for this market to adjust.

Other institutional barriers include licensing and certification requirements. Employers might be willing to lower the standards for a particular occupation, but if entry to the occupation is regulated, the regulatory or licensing board would have to agree. These boards, which are often state bodies, might not wish to lower the standards, and current members of the occupation might object to relaxation because it would cheapen their credentials and possibly result in lower wages. Restrictions on immigration may operate as a similar institutional barrier to achieving equilibrium in occupational labor markets. Trade unions or associations, at the time of contract negotiations or through other activities, may restrict the supply of workers or hiring requirements for workers. An example of this type of barrier is restrictions on the ratio of apprentices to journeyman workers in an occupation. In some instances, such restrictions could constrain employers and potential entrants from increasing the number of entrants in an occupation making use of apprenticeships.

All the barriers mentioned above were established for particular reasons, ostensibly to assure quality for workers in the occupation. Although consideration should be given to changing or eliminating the barriers, their original intent should not be forgotten.

Continuous Increases in Labor Demand

If the labor demand schedule continuously increases faster than the amount supplied can increase, then the market will not achieve equilibrium. This scenario is the basis of the Arrow-Capron dynamic model of labor shortages, and it can occur in periods of rapid sustained growth in one or more industries that employ workers in the shortage occupation. Such a period of sustained rapid growth for a particular sector of the economy can prevent the market from clearing for a substantial period of time. According to Arrow and Capron (1959), this situation occurred for engineers following World War II; more recently, similar rapid growth in demand occurred for information technology (IT) workers in the 1990s in the period leading up to the IT bubble. Note that in this situation the problem is not necessarily that workers or employers cannot adjust; rather, the problem is due to continued shocks to the equilibrium levels of employment and wages.

CONSEQUENCES OF LABOR SHORTAGES

Labor shortages can lead to a number of consequences for the firms experiencing them and the rest of the economy as well. In economic terms, the major consequence of a sustained shortage is that the economy will be operating less efficiently than it could. Until the market achieves equilibrium, resources are not put to their most productive use. Thus, aggregate production for the nation is below capacity. Workers may have to work more hours than they desire, or they may be assigned to jobs they do not want. Employers may have to use their workers and equipment less efficiently than they desire, and this may result in lower output and reduced profits. In some cases, the impact on consumers will be relatively modest, but if consumers cannot obtain needed health care because of a labor shortage, the consequences can be severe. Finally, the impact of a shortage can extend beyond the firms directly experiencing the problem. A shortage of home health workers or nursing home workers, for example, may result in hospitals having to keep patients longer than is desirable or releasing them without adequate care after discharge. Thus, it is difficult to trace all of the effects of an occupational shortage.

By systematically studying occupational labor shortages, and tight labor markets in general, it may be possible to take actions to improve the performance of supporting institutions. As noted at the beginning of the chapter, knowledge about labor shortages can help training institutions, schools, and students make better choices about programs to expand and training programs to enroll in. Identifying occupations with shortages can also be useful for setting government policies regulating entry into occupations and in admitting temporary workers and immigrants.

OUTLINE OF THE REPORT

The remainder of this book has five chapters. The next four chapters provide case studies of special education teachers, pharmacists, physical therapists, and home care workers. For each occupation, we provide background on the occupation, describe the reasons why the occupation was selected for study, and summarize evidence from databases, literature, and interviews on whether the occupation is currently experiencing or recently experienced a labor shortage, the reasons for the shortage, and possible ways to alleviate the shortage. The final chapter provides our conclusions and discusses potential uses for occupational shortage data. More specifically, we discuss the limitations of current occupational data collected by the Bureau of Labor Statistics (BLS) and the extent to which the federal and state governments and other organizations could collect additional data that would be useful for policy purposes. The chapter also discusses how occupational data can be used in immigration policy.

Notes

1. See, for example, Commission on Workforce Quality and Labor Market Efficiency (1989) and Johnston and Packer (1987). For a critical review of this literature, see Barnow and Bawden (1991). For a discussion of how employers in Great Britain distinguish between skill shortages, skill gaps, and hard-to-fill vacancies, see Green, Machin, and Wilkinson (1998).
2. The remainder of this chapter is largely based on work originally presented in Barnow (1996) and Trutko et al. (1993). Many of the references are fairly dated, but some of the most important research on shortages was conducted in the 1950s.
3. This definition, which was provided by the U.S. Department of Labor in a Request for Proposals for a study of labor shortages, is essentially identical to the definition used by Franke and Sobel (1970) in their study of labor shortages: "a situation existing over an extended period of time in which employers were unable to hire at going wages or salaries sufficient numbers of qualified persons to fill positions for which there were budgeted funds and for which personnel were required to meet existing demands for services."
4. Technically, the supply curve for labor may be "backward-bending," which means that at very high wages workers actually reduce the amount of labor they are willing to supply. We do not consider this concept further in our discussion because it is unlikely to be relevant in a study of labor shortages. Labor supply could also be perfectly inelastic, where an increase in the wage rate does not result in an increase in labor supplied. For highly skilled workers, this is often the case in the short run.
5. There are different definitions of labor surpluses as well. For example, in the 1990s, Daniel Hecker of the Bureau of Labor Statistics (1992) concluded that the nation had a surplus of college graduates, whereas Bishop (1996) concluded that there was a shortage. For a review of this issue see Barnow and Bawden (1991).
6. Formally, the internal rate of return is found by solving the equation $0 = (W_0 - C_0) + (W_1 - C_1)/(1 + I) + (W_2 - C_2)/(1 + I)^2 + \ldots + (W_n - C_n)/(1 + I)^n$, where W_t represents earnings in year t, C_t represents costs incurred in year t, and I is the internal rate of return that is solved for.
7. For a similar discussion of the issues raised here, see Burke (2005).
8. This is the situation that occurred in the U.S. labor market for shipfitters in the 1990s. Because shipfitters and oil pipeline workers use many of the same skills, an increase in demand for pipeline workers by the oil companies led to a decrease in the supply of shipfitters (see Trutko and Barnow 1998).
9. The arguments presented above apply primarily to training new hires for entry into an occupation that they are not qualified for. The arguments do not apply, or do not apply to the same extent, to training workers already on the payroll to improve their skills. Moreover, even if training does not pay off for an individual employer, it might result in a return for society as a whole (see Barnow, Chasanov, and Pande 1990).
10. In 1996, TANF replaced Aid to Families with Dependent Children (AFDC).

2
Special Education Teachers

We selected special education teachers as a case study because there have been many reports in the popular and academic literature about shortages in this field, and these reports have persisted for more than 30 years. The labor market for this profession is interesting for several reasons. Although special education teachers are often paid according to the same wage scale as other teachers, they typically have longer and more rigorous training and certification requirements and face a greater number of administrative burdens. Although a shortage of special education teachers could result from rapidly increasing demand, other reasons to explore this occupation include federal and state regulations regarding the provision of special education, limitations on funding possibilities due to the strong role of the public sector in funding special education positions, and institutional rigidities that could be introduced through the collective bargaining process.

BACKGROUND AND DESCRIPTION

Special education teachers work with students who face specific learning disabilities, emotional or behavioral disorders, and physical challenges. The special needs and abilities of these students, who may be emotionally disturbed, learning disabled, mentally retarded, or have speech, hearing, vision, or other impairments, cannot be met well by conventional teaching practices. Special education teachers use a variety of classroom methods to tailor their material to the learning characteristics and needs of their students, usually providing instruction to individuals or small groups (BLS 2010a).

In addition to providing educational instruction, special education teachers have several other responsibilities. First, they are involved in the identification of children with special needs and with the transition of these students between special education and mainstream classes. To this end, they also act as consultants to the entire faculty on issues regarding the transition of children with special needs back into the conventional classroom setting, which is a process of inclusion often referred to as mainstreaming. Second, they serve as advisors to parents of children with special needs, providing counsel on the motivational, cognitive, and social consequences of their children's conditions. Finally, they help to develop an Individualized Education Program (IEP) for each special education student, which sets personalized goals and is tailored to the student's individual needs and ability. This task often includes working with parents, school administrators, and the student's general education teachers to formulate and evaluate long-term strategies to help students attain a sense of social and personal self-sufficiency. Often the special education teacher may work in a resource room, a place where students with mild disabilities may spend a portion of the school day working toward specified goals (BLS 2010a).

The history of special education teaching as a distinct area of teaching is quite brief, beginning in the late 1950s. Prior to that time, special education teachers watered down or simplified regular classroom curricula, an approach that largely reflected a lack of knowledge in the field, as well as a lack of recognition that a different approach was required for the education of children with special needs. In the case of severely disabled students, who were often placed in separate centers or institutions and thus separated from their mainstream peers, teachers focused for the most part on controlling student behavior and attempting to teach students as best they could through conventional instruction methods (Palmer and Hall 1987).

In view of the lack of specialized personnel to train special education teachers, federal legislation was enacted to improve programs and services. Some notable early examples include the establishment of university doctorate-level training programs in the area of mental retardation by the Education of Mentally Retarded Children Act in 1958 (PL 85-926); the Training of Professional Personnel Act of 1959 (PL 86-158), which helped train leaders to educate children with mental retardation; and the Teachers of the Deaf Act of 1961 (PL 87-276), which provided training for instructional personnel for children who were deaf or hard of hearing. In addition, the Elementary and Secondary Education Act of 1965 (PL 89-10) and the State Schools Act of 1965 (PL 89-313) gave states direct grant assistance to help educate children with disabilities. However, in 1970, public schools in the United States educated only one in five children with disabilities because many states had laws excluding certain students from public schools, including children who were deaf, blind, emotionally disturbed, or mentally retarded. Landmark court decisions further advanced educational opportunities for children with disabilities, such as *Pennsylvania Association for Retarded Citizens v. Commonwealth* (1971) and *Mills v. Board of Education of the District of Columbia* (1972), which established the responsibility of states and localities to educate children with disabilities. In these court cases, the right of every child with a disability to be educated was found based on the equal protection clause of the Fourteenth Amendment to the U.S. Constitution (U.S. Department of Education [DOE] 2000).

The enactment of the Education for All Handicapped Children Act (EHA) in 1975 (PL 94-142), which guaranteed a "free and appropriate" education to all disabled children between the ages of 3 and 21, represented a critical turning point both for inclusion of special needs children in regular classroom settings and for creating increased pressure for special education teachers. The four main purposes of the act were 1) to improve how children with disabilities were identified and educated, 2) to evaluate the success of these efforts, 3) to provide due process protections for children and families, and 4) to provide financial incentives to enable states and localities to comply with the EHA. This act affected more than eight million children and greatly increased the demand for special education personnel; in addition, it gave the field an intellectual and professional legitimacy it had not previously enjoyed (Sattler and Sattler 1985). The EHA mandate had several other consequences. First, it stimulated research in the instructional, psychological, and social aspects of special education. Second, it hastened the accumulation and dissemination of new educational methods developed in schools. Finally, it placed the special education teacher at the center of a network of supporting special education personnel (e.g., psychologists, therapists, and social workers), all with the goal of providing an "appropriate" education to children with special needs.

In 1990, the EHA was reauthorized as PL 101-476, the Individuals with Disabilities Education Act (IDEA). The emphasis of the law shifted from a mandate to serve disabled children to the protection of the educational rights of individuals with disabilities. In the same year, the Americans with Disabilities Act (ADA; PL 101-36) was passed. IDEA was amended in 1997, supporting initiatives for transition services from high school to adult living, and the act is periodically reviewed by Congress as part of the Elementary and Secondary School Act. The 1997 amendments emphasized the need to include students with disabilities in state reform efforts, expand the availability of special education classrooms, foster research-based instruction, and support professional development for special educators (Katsiyannis, Zhang, and Conroy 2003).

On December 3, 2004, IDEA was further amended by the Individuals with Disabilities Education Improvement Act of 2004 (PL 108-446), which added the requirement that all public elementary and secondary special education teachers must be "highly qualified" as special education teachers. The definition of "highly qualified special education teachers" in IDEA is aligned with the definition of "highly qualified" general education teachers in the No Child Left Behind Act of 2001 (PL 107-110). In general, to be "highly qualified" requires a special education teacher to have obtained state certification; not to have had state certification waived on an emergency, temporary, or provisional basis; and to hold at least a bachelor's degree (DOE 2007). The many changes to federal legislation over the years helped to shape the requirements for special education teachers. Overall, the passage of the Education for All Handicapped Children Act (later amended to be IDEA) has increased the need for teachers with specialized skills and experience to meet the needs of special education students, who are now guaranteed a free and appropriate education. As is discussed later in this chapter, the "highly qualified" requirement introduces complex questions about whether there is a "quality" shortage—that is, an adequate supply of "highly qualified" special education teachers to meet demand (Boe 2006).

TRAINING AND RECRUITMENT OF WORKERS

This section discusses the educational requirements and qualifications for entry into special education teaching, the factors affecting those requirements, and the methods employers use to fill vacancies in the field. This examination of the means by which individuals enter the occupation lays the groundwork for the later analysis of labor market conditions for special education teachers.

Educational Qualifications and Entry Requirements

In a field with such varied responsibilities and teaching goals, the requirements to enter special education are not uniform by state and are in constant flux. As the goals of special education progressed in the 1960s and 1970s from behavioral control and remedial education to also include emotional and developmental therapy, the proficiencies and skills necessary for a special education teacher expanded well beyond those required for mainstream (general education) teachers.

Entry into special education is primarily regulated by state certification. Not unlike those for general education, the requirements for certification reflect each state's educational philosophy regarding the education of children with special needs, and more recently they have reflected concerns about the adequate supply of qualified special education teachers. As might be expected, there is great variation in state special education standards. However, all 50 states and the District of Columbia require special education teachers to be licensed.

Most states base their certification processes on a few broad premises. First, special education teachers receive a general education credential to teach kindergarten through twelfth grade. Second, these teachers train in a specialty area of special education, such as learning disabilities or behavioral disorders. Third, special education teachers must be able to function as team members and consultants, providing expertise to the general teaching faculty and parents regarding the child's special needs. Finally, special education teachers must be able to assess a pupil's level of functioning and select, implement, and evaluate instructional programs based on each student's individual learning abilities.

A majority of states' certification requirements reflect these fundamental premises. For full certification, all states require a bachelor's degree and completion of an approved teacher preparation program with a prescribed number of subject and education credits. In addition, most states require supervised practice teaching, which is based on the recognition that coteaching with an experienced special education teacher is important in the formation of good instructional skills and habits.

Some states and an increasing number of institutions are also requiring a fifth year of course work, a master's degree in special education, or graduate-level preparation for special education teachers (BLS 2010a). Many states require "dual certification" in special education, meaning that special education teachers are required to obtain a general teaching certificate to qualify for certification in special education.[1] Finally, most states also require a teacher competency test such as the Praxis exam as part of the process of initially certifying all teachers.

A major characteristic of special education certification is the specific category in which it is granted. States may certify special education teachers based upon specific need-based categories, such as autism or speech impairments (categorical certification), or they may certify teachers without strictly defining the areas of special education in which they are qualified to teach (noncategorical and multicategorical certification). Rather than dividing certification according to disability classifications, the noncategorical and multicategorical approaches often specify certification by the level of education or the severity of the disability at which teachers are qualified to teach. A majority of states (27) consider their certification to be noncategorical; however, many of these states also issue certificates in specific categories, such as deafness/hearing impaired, blind/visually impaired, and emotionally disturbed. The remaining states provide categorical certification (Geiger, Crutchfield, and Maizner 2003).

States define categories differently, and they divide special education into various categories. The DOE, in collecting its data on special education programs, collapses this diverse group into 13 broad categories:

1) Specific learning disabilities

2) Speech/language impairments

3) Mental retardation

4) Emotional disturbance

5) Multiple disabilities

6) Hearing impairments

7) Orthopedic impairments

8) Other health impairments

9) Visual impairments

10) Autism

11) Deaf-blindness

12) Traumatic brain injury

13) Developmental delay

A majority of all special education students are in the four larg-est categories: learning-disabled, speech-impaired, mentally retarded, and emotionally disturbed (DOE 2004a). Figure 2.1 shows the broad range of categories for which states provide special education teacher certification.

Although some states hire few uncertified teachers, others report that up to 32 percent of their special education teachers are not fully cer-tified for their main assignments (McLeskey, Tyler, and Flippin 2004).

**Figure 2.1 State Special Education Certification Programs by
        Category Type**

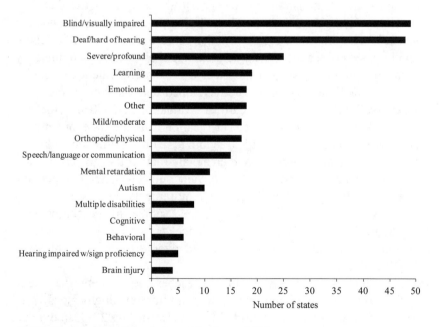

SOURCE: Education Commission of the States (2007).

No Child Left Behind (NCLB) outlines the minimum requirements that "highly qualified" teachers must meet. According to NCLB, a highly qualified teacher must have a bachelor's degree, full state certification, and licensure as defined by the state.

IDEA's most recent amendments, the Individuals with Disabilities Education Improvement Act of 2004, added the requirement that special education teachers must be "highly qualified." The definition of "highly qualified" under IDEA mirrors that of NCLB. However, the "highly qualified" special education teacher requirements apply only to teachers providing direct instruction in core academic subjects. Special education teachers who do not directly instruct students in core academic subjects or who provide only consultation to highly qualified teachers in adapting curricula, using behavioral supports and interventions, or selecting appropriate accommodations do not need to demonstrate subject-matter competency in those subjects (DOE 2004b). This flexibility allows states to have special education teachers who do not meet the "highly qualified" requirements serve as consultants and aides to general education teachers. Additionally, "highly qualified" teachers must also demonstrate competency in the subject matter that they specialize in. Again, this requirement only applies to special education teachers who provide direct instruction in core classes. Middle school and high school teachers must demonstrate their teaching competency with a major in the subject they teach, credits equivalent to a major in the subject, passage of a state-developed test, passage of the High Objective Uniform State Standard of Evaluation (HOUSSE) (for current teachers only), an advanced certification from the state, or a graduate degree.[2] States also have the freedom to define certification, streamline the certification process, and create alternate routes to certification so that current teachers can prove their subject-matter competency and meet "highly qualified" teacher requirements. For example, current teachers may be allowed to prove their subject-matter competency through a mixture of teaching experience, professional development, and knowledge in the subject garnered over time in the profession (DOE 2004b).

By 2006, the "highly qualified" teacher requirements had been revised by each state, and new state plans for revising/personalizing these requirements were submitted for review. In July 2011, individual state plans for amending the "highly qualified" teacher requirements, as well as the reviewer comments, were posted on the Department of Education's Web site (DOE 2011).

Methods Employers Use to Recruit Workers and Workers Use to Obtain Employment

The ability to hire qualified special education teachers in a time of relative teacher scarcity depends on the school or district's ability to attract qualified applicants. This ability is especially vital considering that more than one million teachers are expected to retire in the coming years (DOE 2010). Traditionally, employers, school districts, and private schools have recruited special education teachers in the same way as they did all other teachers, namely by contacting prospective teachers through college or university channels and professional conferences or by placing advertisements in professional publications and newspapers. Word of mouth has also played an important role in attracting teachers. During the 1999–2000 school year, administrators used a variety of strategies to recruit special education teachers. According to an earlier study done by the DOE, 98 percent of school administrators contacted colleges and universities; 97 percent contacted educators in other schools and agencies; 97 percent advertised in local publications; 55 percent contacted teacher organizations; 23 percent advertised in national education publications; and 92 percent recruited in other ways, including Web sites, job fairs, and collaboration with state departments of education (DOE 2002).

The general perception of a tight labor market for special education teachers has led many school districts to devise and implement new strategies to attract and recruit special education teachers. For example, electronic bulletin boards have been developed by a number of education associations listing vacancies available for special education teaching posts around the country. Several state education agencies and associations have also created employment clearinghouses that compile and disseminate employment information about available teaching positions.[3] While these methods will not supplant the traditional recruiting techniques, they have certain advantages. Electronic bulletin boards and employment clearinghouses are accessible to any person or agency across the country, providing greater geographic reach than print newspapers (although Internet-based versions of newspapers offer the same broad coverage). They are less expensive and more up-to-date than professional journals, and they require none of the informal university channels that are inherently limited in range and number. In addition, employment clearinghouses are able to provide prospective applicants with more recruitment material, such as brochures and information on requirements, and to assist applicants in their employment search (Billingsley 2005).

As would be expected, the methods that special education teachers use to seek and obtain positions are generally similar to the methods employers use for recruitment. Teachers use university postings, word of mouth, employment clearinghouses, and computer networks to find vacancies in teaching positions. There is, however, variation in the methods used by different types of applicants. Entrants to special education teaching, newly trained teachers, and those who have recently obtained certification generally rely on university-based channels, professional conferences, job fairs, and journals to seek and obtain teaching positions. With few exceptions, university-based channels are limited geographically to within the state and to states with similar certification procedures.[4] Applicants certified in the field who are reentering the profession and have recently obtained temporary or emergency certification or who have moved from other states are more likely to use employment clearinghouses or employer-based sources of information, primarily because of their lack of other connections.[5]

By the 2008–2009 school year, special education teachers were also being recruited through teaching programs such as Teach for America. This, however, has raised some concern over whether or not these teachers, who are still in the process of becoming certified teachers, meet the "highly qualified" requirement and have the experience necessary to offer specialized education (Langland 2009). It also further highlights the significant hardship school systems across the country are facing in finding and retaining qualified candidates to fill vacancies for special education teaching opportunities.

WORKER CHARACTERISTICS

Broad national data on the demographic characteristics of special education teachers show some similarities between special and general education teachers, but they also highlight several distinct characteristics. According to the Study of Personnel Needs in Special Education (SPeNSE), a one-time detailed survey of special education teachers, the following differences exist (Carlson et al. 2002):

- Special education teachers are more likely to be women compared to general education teachers—in 2000, 85 percent of special education teachers were female, compared to 76 percent of general education teachers.

- In terms of race, there are relatively slight differences between special education and general education teachers—in 2000, 86 percent of special education teachers were white, compared to 88 percent of general education teachers; 4 percent of special education teachers were Hispanic, while 7 percent of general education teachers were Hispanic.

- A greater percentage of special education teachers are disabled as compared to general education teachers: 14 percent of special education teachers reported a disability in 2000, compared to 6 percent of general education teachers.

- The average age for both special and general education teachers is about the same—in 2000, the average age for both types of teachers was 43 years.

- Special education teachers tend to be slightly less experienced than general education teachers—in 2000, special education teachers had an average of 14.3 years of experience compared to 15.5 years of experience for general education teachers.

- Special education teachers are considerably more likely to have an advanced degree. In 2000, 59 percent of special education teachers had their master's degree compared to 49 percent of general education teachers. However, special education teachers were less likely than general education teachers to be fully certified for their main teaching assignment; in 2000, 92 percent of special education teachers were fully certified compared to 95 percent of general education teachers. In addition, only 71 percent of beginning special education teachers, those with less than three years of experience, were fully certified for their main assignment.

Special education teachers' characteristics also vary somewhat by type of teacher, geographical region, type of school, and other factors. For example, special education teachers serving younger students tend to have less experience (13.3 years compared to the average of 14.3 years), and special education teachers in urban areas tend to have more years of experience than their counterparts in suburban and rural areas (15.2 years compared to 13.8 and 14 years, respectively).

EMPLOYMENT AND EARNINGS TRENDS

Employment Trends

Employment levels and change

As with the growth in students receiving special education services, there has been rapid growth in the number of special education teachers. Table 2.1 shows the trends in the number of special education teachers compared to general education teachers and all workers from 2006 to 2010. From 2006 to 2010, the number of special education teachers (preschool, kindergarten, elementary, middle, and secondary) increased by 3 percent, from 455,220 to 468,850. In comparison, the number of general education teachers (preschool, kindergarten, elementary, middle, and secondary) increased by 0.4 percent over the same period, from 3,720,040 to 3,736,540. Middle school special education teachers and general education preschool, kindergarten, and elementary school teachers had the lowest growth in employment from 2006 to 2010, at a rate of −0.9 percent for middle school special education teachers and −0.4 percent for general education preschool, kindergarten, and elementary school teachers. Overall, special education teacher employment has grown at a faster rate than general education teachers, and at a much faster rate than all workers in all occupations (−4.2 percent). Spe-

Table 2.1 Number of and Percentage Change in Employment for Special Education Teachers and Other Occupations, 2006–2010

Occupation	2006	2007	2008	2009	2010	% change
Special education teachers						
Preschool, kindergarten, elementary school	216,930	219,930	226,250	228,580	226,920	4.6
Middle school	101,420	100,160	100,650	102,490	100,510	−0.9
Secondary school	136,870	141,330	147,210	146,240	141,420	3.3
Total	455,220	461,420	474,110	477,310	468,850	3.0
General education teachers						
Preschool, kindergarten, elementary school	2,036,560	2,089,840	2,110,970	2,115,770	2,028,310	−0.4
Middle school	652,700	652,560	661,820	665,420	655,090	0.4
Secondary school	1,030,780	1,058,870	1,090,490	1,091,710	1,053,140	2.2
Total	3,720,040	3,801,270	3,863,280	3,872,900	3,736,540	0.4
All education, training, and library occupations	8,206,440	8,316,360	8,451,250	8,488,740	8,457,870	3.1
All workers from all occupations	132,604,980	134,354,250	135,185,230	130,647,610	127,097,160	−4.2

SOURCE: 2006–2009 data: BLS (2011a); 2010 data: BLS (2011b).

cial education teacher employment has also grown at about the same rate as all education, training, and library occupations (although growth has been fastest among preschool, kindergarten, and elementary and secondary school special education teachers).

Unemployment trends

Another key indicator of labor market conditions is the annual average unemployment rate by occupation. Occupations experiencing shortages, in which the number of vacancies is significantly greater than the number of qualified applicants, are likely to have very low unemployment rates, since those searching for jobs find them quickly and are thus unemployed for a very short period (Cohen 1990). Table 2.2 illustrates the trend in the annual unemployment rate for special education teachers, postsecondary teachers, preschool and kindergarten teachers, elementary and middle school teachers, secondary school teachers, and all workers from all occupations. The annual unemployment rate for special education teachers averaged nearly 1.9 percent between 2006 and 2010, compared to 2.7 percent for postsecondary teachers, 3.7 percent for preschool and kindergarten teachers, 2.9 percent for elementary and middle school teachers, and 1.9 percent for secondary school teachers. The unemployment rate in this period for all workers from

Table 2.2 Average Annual Unemployment Rate (%) for Special Education Teachers, General Education Teachers, and All Workers, 2006–2010

Occupation	2006	2007	2008	2009	2010
Special education teachers	1.40	1.40	1.00	2.90	2.90
Postsecondary teachers	2.10	2.50	2.80	3.20	3.10
Preschool and kindergarten teachers	2.90	2.90	3.00	4.50	5.10
Elementary and middle school teachers	2.00	2.10	2.30	3.90	4.10
Secondary school teachers	1.50	1.30	1.60	2.40	2.50
All education, training, and library occupations	2.40	2.30	2.80	4.10	4.20
All workers from all occupations	4.20	4.20	5.30	8.60	8.90

SOURCE: Unpublished BLS data from the Current Population Survey (2006–2010), Table 3: Annual average employed and experienced unemployed persons by detailed occupation and class of worker.

all occupations was 6.2 percent. Across all years, with the exception of secondary school teachers, special education teachers had consistently lower unemployment rates, ranging from a high of 2.9 percent in 2009 and 2010 to a low of 1.0 percent in 2008. Although the low unemployment rates for special education teachers indicate a tight labor market and are consistent with the presence of a shortage, they do not necessarily prove that there is a shortage within the occupation.

Projections for future employment growth within the occupation

Although special education teacher employment growth has been occurring at a faster pace over the past five years than that of general education teachers (as shown in Table 2.1), the BLS projections for employment growth from 2010 through 2018 (Table 2.3) suggest that the percentage increase in special education teachers (18.2 percent) will likely be less than that for general education teachers (20.1 percent). The increase for special education teachers is also projected to be at

Table 2.3 Employment Projections: Special Education Teachers, General Education Teachers, and All Workers, 2010 and Projected 2018

Occupation	2010	Projected 2018	% change
Special education teachers			
Preschool, kindergarten, elementary school	226,920	270,000	19.0
Middle school	100,510	118,000	17.4
Secondary school	141,420	166,000	17.4
Total	468,850	554,000	18.2
General education teachers			
Preschool, kindergarten, elementary school	2,028,310	2,544,000	25.4
Middle school	655,090	761,000	16.2
Secondary school	1,053,140	1,184,000	12.4
Total	3,736,540	4,489,000	20.1
All education, training, and library occupations	8,457,870	10,534,000	24.5
All workers from all occupations	127,097,160	166,206,000	30.8

SOURCE: BLS (2010a).

a slower pace through 2018 in comparison to all education, training, and library occupations (24.5 percent) and all workers (30.8 percent). Within the special education field, the percentage increase in employment is expected to be slightly faster among preschool, kindergarten, and elementary school teachers (19.0 percent) versus middle school and secondary school teachers (both 17.4 percent). Overall, the slower rate of growth in employment for special education teachers versus general education teachers and all workers is not generally considered indicative of future labor shortages (i.e., as opposed to if very fast growth in employment was expected within a field).

Supply and demand conditions (as indicated by survey results)

The American Association for Employment in Education (AAEE) conducts an annual survey titled Educator Supply and Demand in the United States. AAEE surveys educators in colleges and universities and career services nationwide to analyze the demand for teachers and subdivides the results into 11 geographic regions. Each field can be classified into one of five areas based on the measurable demand: 1) considerable shortage, 2) some shortage, 3) balanced, 4) some surplus, and 5) considerable surplus. Table 2.4 shows the results of AAEE's 2010 survey, which indicate that there was an imbalance between demand and supply within most specialty areas of special education teaching in 2010. As shown in the table, within most of the special education fields, there was what survey respondents judged to be either considerable shortage or somewhat of a shortage. By region, the survey respondents reported the following labor market conditions for special education teachers:

- Region 1 consists of Idaho, Oregon, and Washington. A mix of considerable and some shortages in special education fields is present.

- Region 2 consists of Arizona, California, Nevada, and Utah. A mix of considerable and some shortages is present for all special education fields.

- Region 3 includes Colorado, Montana, New Mexico, and Wyoming. A considerable shortage is found for all fields of special education, except for the multicategorical field, where there is some shortage.

Table 2.4 AAEE Shortage Findings by Special Education Field and Region, 2010

Special education field	Region of the country										
	1	2	3	4	5	6	7	8	9	10	11
Multicategorical	4.36	3.91	4.14	4.12	3.88	4.06	4.06	3.73	4.21	5.00	4.67
Emotional/behavioral disorders	4.00	4.27	4.43	4.16	4.00	4.07	4.09	3.74	4.09	—	4.50
Hearing-impaired	3.57	4.11	4.50	3.96	4.07	3.85	3.95	3.93	4.22	—	4.50
Learning disability	3.86	4.09	4.29	4.03	4.00	3.92	3.85	3.77	4.10	—	4.50
Mental retardation	3.71	4.22	4.29	4.03	4.06	4.00	4.07	3.84	4.18	—	4.50
Visually impaired	3.71	4.14	4.29	4.04	4.13	3.84	3.97	3.96	4.11	—	4.50
Mild/moderate disabilities	4.13	4.25	4.29	4.16	4.06	3.98	4.00	3.70	4.20	—	5.00
Severe/profound disabilities	4.00	4.50	4.29	4.21	4.13	4.05	4.28	3.86	4.17	—	5.00
Early childhood special education	3.86	4.18	4.50	3.97	3.94	3.68	3.64	3.65	4.14	5.00	4.00
Dual certificate (general/special education)	4.11	4.09	4.25	4.03	3.88	3.98	3.90	3.72	4.21	5.00	4.67

NOTE: 5.00–4.21: considerable shortage; 4.20–3.41: some shortage; and 3.40–2.61: balance. See the text for states included in each region.
SOURCE: American Association for Employment in Education (2010).

- Region 4 is comprised of Iowa, Kansas, Minnesota, Missouri, Nebraska, North Dakota, and South Dakota. Some shortage is present for all fields except in the severe/profound disabilities field of special education, in which considerable shortage is found.

- Region 5 consists of Arkansas, Louisiana, Oklahoma, and Texas. Some shortage is found in all fields of special education.

- Region 6 contains Alabama, Florida, Georgia, Kentucky, Mississippi, North Carolina, South Carolina, Tennessee, Virginia, and West Virginia. Some shortage is present for all fields of special education.

- Region 7 includes Illinois, Indiana, Michigan, Ohio, and Wisconsin. A considerable shortage is present for the severe/profound disabilities field, and some shortage is present for all other fields.

- Region 8 consists of Delaware, the District of Columbia, Maryland, New Jersey, New York, and Pennsylvania. Some shortage is present for all fields of special education.

- Region 9 includes Connecticut, Maine, Massachusetts, New Hampshire, Rhode Island, and Vermont. Some shortage is present in this region for all fields except for hearing-impaired, multicategorical, and dual certificate, where there is considerate shortage present.

- Region 10 consists of Alaska. A considerable shortage is present in the three fields of special education provided.

- Region 11 consists of Hawaii. A considerable shortage is present for all fields of special education except for early childhood special education, where there is some shortage present.

Earnings Trends

The relative wage rate change in an occupation is often an important indicator of labor market dynamics, especially in the short run. In occupations where market forces move freely (i.e., supply, demand, and wages are not regulated by the government), a rapid rise in wages may indicate the presence of a shortage. Wages in special education, as with many occupations substantially supported by government funding, do not necessarily behave in this manner. It is important nevertheless to observe the trends in mean annual salaries for special education, as compared to other professions. Table 2.5 shows the mean annual earnings in the United States for special education teachers for the period from 2006 to 2010, in comparison with general education teachers and all workers from all occupations. The changes in mean annual earnings for special education teachers over the five-year period are not all that different from trends for general education teachers and slightly less than the gains for all workers from all occupations. Earning changes for middle-school special education teachers (7.7 percent) lagged behind those for both preschool, kindergarten, and elementary-school special education teachers (11.1 percent) and secondary-school special education teachers (10.6 percent). Despite roughly comparable change in earnings over the five-year period, the actual mean earnings of special education teachers (ranging from $55,220 for preschool, kindergarten, and elementary teachers to $58,080 for secondary school teachers) were higher in 2010 than the mean earnings for general education teachers in each of the three teacher categories (ranging from $45,027 for preschool, kindergarten, and elementary teachers to $55,990 for secondary school teachers). Earnings for special education teachers were also quite a bit higher (by slightly more than 25 percent) than those for all workers from all occupations ($44,410) in 2010.

In terms of detecting the presence of shortages within an occupation, wages themselves are generally not as important as how they change over time, especially relative to those for other related professions. Economic theory generally suggests that rapidly rising earnings are a possible indicator of tight labor market conditions (and in some cases, shortages) in freely moving labor markets, but in the case of teachers, free movement of wages is restricted by government-negotiated pay scales. Overall, the pace of change in mean annual earnings for special education teachers as shown in Table 2.5 is not all that different from that of general education teachers and, hence, does not seem to signal a strong likelihood of labor market tightness.

Although changes in earnings for special education teachers nationally over the past five years are not broadly indicative of shortages, it is possible that there are specific regions of the country where labor mar-

54

Table 2.5 Mean Annual Earnings ($) and Percentage Change, 2006–2010

Occupation	2006	2007	2008	2009	2010	% change
Special education teachers						
Preschool, kindergarten, elementary school	49,710	51,230	52,970	53,770	55,220	11.1
Middle school	52,550	51,610	53,540	54,750	56,600	7.7
Secondary school	52,520	53,020	55,050	56,420	58,080	10.6
General education teachers						
Preschool, kindergarten, elementary school	40,547	41,197	42,873	43,660	45,027	11.0
Middle school	49,470	50,630	52,570	53,550	54,880	10.9
Secondary school	51,150	52,450	54,390	55,150	55,990	9.5
All education, training, and library occupations	45,320	46,610	48,460	49,530	50,440	11.3
All workers from all occupations	39,190	40,690	42,270	43,460	44,410	13.3

SOURCE: BLS (2011a).

ket conditions are tight and where wage levels (and changes over time) are quite different from national trends. For special education teachers, salary and attrition rates are strongly negatively correlated at the state level, particularly at the top and bottom of salary distribution scales. Like general education teachers, special education teachers move in and out of lower paying jobs in urban areas more quickly because opportunities for higher salaries in nearby districts are often abundant. In addition, special education teachers move into employment outside of teaching when working conditions and wages are better (Brownell et al. 2002).

LABOR MARKET FACTORS CONTRIBUTING TO A SHORTAGE

This section assesses the most prominent factors on the demand and supply sides that have been cited as affecting labor market conditions for special education teachers. The factors discussed have been singled out in interviews conducted as part of this study (with individuals from associations and academia knowledgeable about special education teacher trends), as well as in the extensive literature on special education teachers.

Demand-Side Factors

Growth in size of student-age and special needs population

Growth of the student-age population and the special needs population, in particular, has led to a rise in the demand for special education teachers. This is a key demand-side factor cited in both the literature and in our interviews conducted as part of this study. For example, one study interviewee observed, "There has been an increase in the number of students identified, diagnosed, and categorized as in need of special education . . . There is growing demand for special education due in part to increased diagnoses." The nation's student-age population grew significantly through the 1990s and 2000s. In addition, the students in need of special education assistance grew even faster than the overall student population, which created increased demand for special education teachers. Based on data collected for the 28th Annual Report to Congress by the DOE (2006), Table 2.6 presents trends in the school-age population in comparison to the number of special education students in the 50 states and the District of Columbia from 1995 to 2004. From 1995 to 2004, the total population aged 6 through 21 grew by 9.6 percent, while the students served under IDEA aged 6 to 21 grew at the much higher rate of 19.8 percent. The number of students receiving special education services increased every year during this period at an average annual rate of about 2.3 percent, while the total population aged 6 to 21 grew at a much slower pace (1.2 percent) over the same time period.

Medical technological advancement

The American Association of School Administrators believes that the rapid growth in the number of children in need of and receiving special education assistance is due in part to developments in medical technology (Berman and Urion 2003). Children who would have previously perished from premature births or infant illnesses are now more likely to survive. However, these children often have more medical complications and conditions such as cerebral palsy and borderline mental retardation. They matriculate into public education systems under special needs categories. In addition, medical technology can diagnose conditions such as autism and behavioral disorders at a higher rate than in the past. As a result, school enrollment for children with forms of autism and special needs has increased. States such as Massachusetts, California, and New York report an increase in special needs students with these conditions (Fox News 2007).

Deinstitutionalization and mainstreaming of special needs children

As discussed earlier in this chapter, since the mid-1970s, there have been a series of federal laws enacted (including IDEA in 2004) that have tightened and made more explicit requirements for serving children with disabilities within the public education system. Deinstitutionalization of special needs children, a product of federal legislation and requirements enacted since 1975, created a shift away from state institutions and toward programs provided by schools and communities (Ber-

Table 2.6 Students Receiving Special Education Services, Aged 6–21, 1995–2004

Year	Total served under IDEA Part B aged 6–21	Total population aged 6–21	Students receiving special education services (%)	Change in students receiving special education services (%)	Change in total population aged 6–21 (%)
1995	5,036,139	60,109,523	8.4	—	—
1996	5,185,444	61,339,104	8.5	2.96	2.05
1997	5,347,058	62,552,035	8.5	3.12	1.98
1998	5,486,630	63,763,580	8.6	2.61	1.94
1999	5,620,764	64,717,510	8.7	2.44	1.50
2000	5,711,482	65,383,159	8.7	1.61	1.03
2001	5,797,930	65,790,897	8.8	1.51	0.62
2002	5,892,878	65,896,444	8.9	1.64	0.16
2003	5,970,497	65,885,462	9.1	1.32	−0.02
2004	6,033,425	65,871,265	9.2	1.05	−0.02

SOURCE: DOE (2006).

man and Urion 2003). The creation of IEPs and the matriculation of formerly institutionalized students into public education systems created a need for more special needs educators and support staff. Exceptional students must be placed in the "least restrictive environment" in which they can effectively learn. The least restrictive requirement is aimed at preventing unnecessary segregation/institutionalization of students with disabilities. As a result, most students with mild disabilities spend all or most of their day in a general education setting and may be assigned a full- or part-time instructional assistant to help them with assignments. If a student is not able to learn in a general instruction classroom, the student may be placed in a more restrictive setting in which the student participates in the general education setting for a portion of the day, but receives most academic instruction in a separate classroom from a special education teacher or other staff. Students unable to function within a general education or special education classroom may receive instruction at home or be placed at a school specializing in providing instruction to children with specific and more serious disabling conditions. The highest level of restrictive placement—one in which very few students with disabilities are placed today—is a residential (or institutional) placement. The overall effect of the requirement to provide "free and appropriate public education" in the least restrictive environment (i.e., mainstreaming) is to increase the number of students with disabilities served within the public school system, thereby increasing overall demand for special education teachers. It should, however, be noted that public schools have had a long time to adjust to mainstreaming of children with disabilities (the Education for All Handicapped Children Act made special education programs mandatory in the mid-1970s) and should have made the necessary adjustments over time to deal with legislative and regulatory changes.

Class size

The demand for special education teachers is affected by student-teacher ratios, with a declining ratio of students per teacher necessitating an increase in the number of teachers (if the total number of students remains constant or rises). The demand for special education teachers is governed overall by an array of federal and state legislation that mandates "a free and appropriate" education for children with disabilities.

To comply with these requirements, state and local education authorities have developed guidelines to control how the needs of children with disabilities are to be "appropriately" met, including establishing student-teacher ratios for children with various disabilities. A portion of the demand for teachers that may go unfilled may be related to reducing student-teacher ratios over time. Boe (2006), for example, observes that one factor driving demand for special education teachers—particularly for special education teachers serving young children with disabilities—has been decreasing student-teacher ratios:

> The number of students per teaching position for the 3–5 age group declined from a ratio of 27.2:1 in 1989/1990 to a ratio of 17.5:1 in 2000/2001 (before increasing to 22.6:1 2 years later). In contrast, the comparable ratio for the 6–21 age group held remarkably steady, at close to 15:1 throughout the 15-year period studied. Thus, the shortage of SETs [special education teachers] for students aged 3–5 years with disabilities might be explained, in part, by efforts to rapidly reduce the student-teacher ratio, thereby putting extraordinary pressure on sources of supply. But the same explanation does not apply to the shortage of SETs for students aged 6–21 years, since the student-teacher ratio was stable, at approximately 15:1, during the 15-year period examined. (p. 145)

Supply-Side Factors

"Highly qualified" teaching requirement

During interviews conducted for this study, several respondents highlighted the role that increased certification requirements have played—especially the "highly qualified" requirement—as a supply-side factor in contributing to a tight market for special education teachers. As discussed earlier, the reauthorization of IDEA in 2004 added the requirement that special education teachers must be highly qualified, which aligns special education teaching with NCLB. According to 34 CFR 300.18(b)(1), the following three conditions must be met for a special education teacher to be considered highly qualified:

1) The teacher has obtained full state certification as a special education teacher (including certification obtained through alternative routes to certification), or passed the state special education

teacher licensing examination, and holds a license to teach in the state as a special education teacher. When used with respect to any teacher in a public charter school, highly qualified means that the teacher meets the certification or licensing requirements, if any, set forth in the state's public charter school law.

2) The teacher has not had special education certification or licensure requirements waived on an emergency, temporary, or provisional basis.

3) The teacher holds at least a bachelor's degree.

The highly qualified teacher requirement has added another hurdle for administrators in the education field to recruit and retain highly qualified teachers, which has led to the rise in alternative certification programs and, in some cases, the use of uncertified teachers in the classroom.

Interviewees pointed to the importance of legislation increasing requirements for special education teachers as the key underlying factor in the tight labor market for special education teachers. For example, one interviewee observed the following about tightening certification requirements for special education teachers:

> IDEA tightened eligibility requirements to become a special education teacher, in particular, the "highly qualified" requirements, which have resulted in shortages of special education teachers. The "full inclusion" philosophy was a factor with regard to shortages in the 1990s—but this factor has been sidelined since the enactment of the highly qualified requirement. Some special education teachers had been working in self-contained classrooms, but when the new definition came along, some of these special education teachers were no longer considered highly qualified. As a result, they needed to pass tests or became floaters that did not teach in core content areas. This was very demoralizing, and often special education teachers were not happy because of their new floating consultant-like positions.

Cook and Boe (2007) have pointed to the need for careful analyses of two types of demand for special education teachers, one of which ("quality demand") has resulted in shortfalls of fully qualified special education teachers:

Examination of the adequacy of teacher supply requires a distinction between two types of teacher demand and the adequacy of supply in relation to each type including: (a) quantity demand, or the demand for the *number of* teachers to fill all teaching positions that have been created and funded at the district level, and (b) quality demand, or the demand for teachers with specific *qualifications* such as certification level, certification field, amount of teacher preparation, and degree major field. (p. 218)

In their analyses, Cook and Boe (2007) found there was a need to replace 49,000 less-than-fully-certified special education teachers (practicing in 2001–2002) and that the shortfall of fully certified special education teachers had been growing each year since 1993. The authors conclude, "There is an enormous unmet need for qualified SETs [special education teachers] that is unlikely to be met in the near future regardless of modest increases in the production of new teachers and recruitment from other available sources."

The distinction raised by Cook and Boe (2007) between quantity and quality illustrates the difficulties in defining an occupational shortage. Most of the literature indicates that the vast majority of special education students are being taught, even if not by "highly qualified" special education teachers. Thus, the market is clearing in the sense that school districts are responding to the lack of highly qualified special education teachers and employing other individuals. This is no different than the standard response we would expect from employers facing a tight labor market—while they would prefer to have workers with the best possible credentials, they will accept others when the alternative is to have untaught classes or to cram many more students into classes with highly qualified teachers. This is not to suggest that there is not a serious problem in the special education labor market—to the contrary, the recognition that many classes are taught by teachers who are not highly qualified signifies that there is a problem in attracting and retaining highly qualified individuals; the problem is akin to the social demand shortage concept introduced by Arrow and Capron (1959).

Attrition

High rates of attrition are, in the literature, an often-cited factor affecting the supply of special education teachers. Attrition was also identified as a key factor by a number of experts interviewed for this study and often linked to several other factors affecting supply, including extra administrative burden, working conditions, and lack of a pay differential versus general education teachers. For example, one interviewee makes this observation:

> If changes are not made in No Child Left Behind (NCLB) and IDEA, it can be expected that in the future, shortages will get worse. This is because lots of teachers working in special education will age out (an estimated 50 percent of special education teachers are ready to or are eligible for retirement); also, not as many new special education teachers are coming in and staying in the field as they are likely to leave within the first five years. Among new special education teachers, an estimated 50 percent leave within first five years, so overall, it is not possible to replenish those who are retiring and leaving the field of special education.

The literature that examines key factors determining whether there is an adequate supply of special education teachers focuses considerably on retention and attrition of special education teachers. In a critical analysis of the research literature, Billingsley (2004) observes the following:

> Although the causes of the shortage problem are complex, teacher attrition is clearly a major contributor. Recent evidence suggests that special education, math, and science are the fields with the highest turnover and that special education teachers are more likely to depart than any other teacher group (Ingersoll 2001). McLeskey et al. (2004) provide an analysis of the research on special education attrition rates and suggest that a greater proportion of special educators than general educators leave. (p. 39)

Several types of attrition have been examined in the literature, including leaving the teaching profession altogether and transferring to other teaching and educational positions. Of particular interest has been the loss of special education teachers to general education, with some researchers reporting a higher proportion of special education teachers transferring to general education than the reverse (Boe et al. 1996).

The research demonstrates that teacher characteristics and work factors play critical roles in determining special educators' job satisfaction and career decisions. Billingsley (2004) provides an overview in a review of the literature of four key characteristics and personal factors that influence teachers' decisions to leave special education:

(1) Younger and inexperienced special educators are more likely to leave than their older, more experienced counterparts; (2) uncertified teachers are more likely to leave than certified teachers; (3) special educators with higher test scores (e.g., on the National Teacher Exam) are more likely to leave; and (4) teachers' personal circumstances (e.g., family move, decision to stay home with children) often contribute to attrition. (p. 50)

Despite the attention that attrition has received, not all researchers agree that attrition and teacher retention are key determinants of the balance between supply and demand of special education teachers. Boe, Cook, and Sunderland (2008) assert that teacher attrition in special education in the 1990s appeared to be equivalent in magnitude to that in general education:

Attrition percentage of SETs [special education teachers] and GETs [general education teachers] during the 1990s (aggregated) was comparable (about 10%), but clearly less than that from all nonbusiness occupations (about 13%) . . . Thus, there is no evidence that public school teachers left their LEA [local education authority] of employment at a higher rate than did employees from nonbusiness employers nationally. In fact, the corporate attrition rate of public teachers was actually lower than for nonbusiness occupations during the 1990s. (p. 17)

Boe and Cook (2006) find that what they term "total annual turnover" (i.e., the sum of attrition, teaching area transfer, and school migration) of special education and general education teachers increased substantially during the period from 1991–1992 to 2000–2001. However, based on aggregated data for 1991–1992, 1994–1995, and 2000–2001, the total annual turnover of public school teachers was virtually identical for both groups of teachers (22.8 percent of special education teachers and 22.4 percent of general education teachers left teaching, switched teaching area, or migrated to a different school annually during the 1990s). The authors found some differences between the two groups in the extent of various types of turnover: special education teachers were somewhat less likely to switch teaching areas than general education teachers, but they were somewhat more likely to change schools. In a related study, Boe, Cook, and Sunderland (2008) note that teacher turnover rates are more similar than different for special education and general education teachers and conclude the following:

Our conclusions from this research are that teacher attrition is not excessive in comparison with other vocations and that retention will not improve substantially unless prevailing conditions improve dramatically. This is unlikely; therefore, the supply of qualified teachers needs to be increased sufficiently to satisfy demand. Although the topic of teacher supply is too large and complex to be reviewed here (see Cook and Boe 2007; Curran and Abrahams 2000; Snyder et al. 2006), we use special education to illustrate the need for enhanced supply. Of first-time SETs [special education teachers] hired in 1999–2000, only 46% were extensively prepared to teach in special education; the others were either prepared in general education or had inadequate preparation. (p. 27)

Administrative burden/working conditions

Both our interviews and the literature point to excessive administrative burden and working conditions—without additional compensation—as a potential key factor with regard to difficulty in recruitment of new teachers into the special education field as well as a major precipitating factor for existing special education teachers making a switch to general education teaching or moving out of teaching altogether. For example, one interviewee pointed directly to working conditions as an underlying factor in attrition: "Working conditions are a major cause of shortages of special education teachers. As you might suspect, special education teachers have unworkable caseloads and face unrealistic demands . . . when you have role ambiguity it leads to burnout. Special education teachers have too much paperwork."

As a result of NCLB, special education teachers are sometimes placed as consultants in general education classrooms or used as resources. Without their own classes in their specialized fields of special education, many have high caseloads, must complete a great deal of paperwork, and travel around the school building to complete different tasks. Also as a result of NCLB, all the students with special education needs are required to take state assessments, which can be time-consuming to administer and score. The result is a workload increase for special education teachers, which coupled with the redefined teaching role has led to increased burnout and attrition. As noted in the previous section of this report, attrition is a major concern for the special education teacher labor market (Billingsley 2005).

SPeNSE identified the paperwork burden related to monitoring student progress and the paperwork associated with IDEA policy changes as the leading causes of burnout for special education teachers (DOE 2002). In her analysis of studies investigating the factors that contribute to special education teacher attrition and retention, Billingsley (2004) found stress to be one of the most powerful predictors of attrition. Billingsley (2004) emphasizes the connection between stress and school climate, "role" problems, and paperwork. In inadequate work environments, in which special educators lacked necessary materials, experienced poor administrative support, and dealt with low staff morale, teachers were more likely to leave their positions. Role problems (including role overload, role conflict and ambiguity, and role dissonance) create stress and decrease job satisfaction for special educators. In one study Billingsley reviewed, 68 percent of special education teachers felt that they had too little time to do their work, and nearly 33 percent found conflicting goals and directions to be a frequent source of stress (Morvant and Gersten 1995, cited in Billingsley 2004). In addition, several studies found that paperwork is significantly related to intent to leave teaching, and 60 percent of teachers who planned to leave urban school districts cited paperwork problems as a major factor in their decision (Billingsley 2004).

ASSESSMENT OF LABOR MARKET/SHORTAGE CONDITIONS

Interviewees for this study and recent literature both suggest that the labor market for special education teachers is tight and that there appear to be an insufficient number of fully qualified special education teachers to fill vacancies. In addition, analysts observe that there are certain geographic areas and subspecialties within the special education field where school districts face serious challenges to filling vacancies, especially with personnel that meet certification requirements under IDEA.

Interviewees for this study were in agreement that there have been long-standing shortfalls of fully qualified special education teachers to fill job vacancies. As a result, in some instances, school districts "lower the bar" to fill vacancies with less than fully certified teachers. Several of the interviewees indicated that school districts have faced shortages of special education teachers dating back to the mid-1970s. For example, according to one interviewee, "There has never not been a shortage since 1974. Special education teachers have been a critical shortage area since the inception of the legislation mandating free and appropriate education to all disabled children (i.e., since PL 94-142 went into effect). At the time the legislation was enacted, there was a rush to get special education teachers certified." A second interviewee observed, "Special education teachers actually have a relatively short history as a profession—with the passage of PL 94-142 (in 1974), there was an immediate shortage and there have been continuing shortages since." A third interviewee was unsure when shortages first arose, but observed labor market conditions had "worsened" as a result of the "highly qualified" definition incorporated into IDEA in 2004.

Interviewees highlighted shortage or near-shortage conditions in certain geographical areas, notably inner city and rural areas, and certain regions of the country. They cited a variety of factors for geographic differences in shortage conditions, including lack of mobility, pay differentials, and working conditions. For example, one interviewee observed the following geographic trends and underlying factors driving the trends:

> There are some areas with better supply than others, but hardly any inner city or rural areas are exempt from these shortages. There are areas of the Midwest that have the least amount of need and best supply of special education teachers—for example, Wisconsin, Iowa, Michigan, Indiana, and Iowa have lots of preparation programs. Also, Pennsylvania prepares lots of special education teachers . . . While there is sometimes a problem with reciprocity between states in accepting special education teachers' certifications, the bigger problem is that people do not want to move away (from where they grew up) to take teaching jobs in other states. While people might go to another state to go to college and receive a special education teaching degree, they usually want to go back home to teach. This is why our organization is introducing community-based teaching campaigns.

A second interviewee observed that there is variation across states and localities because of differences in working conditions, pay, and the highly diverse Title I populations. He noted that urban and rural areas are having the most trouble attracting well-qualified special education teachers (and teachers in general) and that problems of shortages of special education teachers tend not to be as bad in wealthier suburban areas. He also noted that, as a result, about half of special education teachers in many large cities are teaching under emergency licensure. He went on to observe that pay differentials can make a critical difference locally from school district to school district:

> Affluent stable school districts are often able to steal people from surrounding districts; some districts also set salary scales so it is possible to attract teachers from out of state. No state has been able to deal with the "equitable" distribution requirement in NCLB (which calls for equal distribution of SE [special education] teachers across the state). If you paid special education teachers more, over time the shortage would be reduced . . . if (for example) pay was $100,000 for special education teachers, the shortages would largely go away.

Interviewees also highlighted tight labor market conditions for certain subspecialties within special education teaching. One interviewee noted that shortages are worst for those teachers that teach children with specific types of disabilities, citing long-term shortages (20 years or more) of special education teachers for the visually impaired. He also noted more recent shortages related to special education teachers that are qualified to teach specific content areas (e.g., reading/math), with the challenge being that special education teachers need to meet more requirements than a general education teacher (i.e., they need to meet both subject content and special education requirements). A second interviewee also highlighted the difficulties that some school districts encountered in filling specialty areas within special education:

- Shortage areas change somewhat from year to year. Those consistently at the top in terms of shortages are: teachers of severely and profoundly disabled children, emotionally disturbed children, and multicategorical children (i.e., many of these children spend one-half their time in general education classrooms and teachers must be able to handle multiple disabilities). As states move to a multicategorical model, you need to get more teachers qualified to teach in more than one environment.

- Shortages of special education teachers of the visually impaired (VI) are increasing . . . because there are not enough preparation programs distributed across the nation (many states do not have a VI preparation program).

- Low-incidence disabilities have a good pool/supply, and teachers do not leave the field; the problem is that there may not be many training programs in the state or locality for this type of teacher. However, there is a revolving door (high attrition) for teachers of emotionally disabled and severe and profoundly disabled.

Finally, a third interviewee highlighted challenges in recruiting and keeping special education teachers serving those students that are the most difficult and demanding to serve: "Special education teachers for the emotionally disabled/disturbed is where the shortages are the greatest—it is the area where teaching is least reinforcing and most segregated—this group of students is the hardest to work with."

The literature indicates that the labor market has been and continues to be tight for special education teachers, especially when it comes to fully certified teachers. Boe summarizes labor market conditions in the 1990s and how, in the early 2000s, the concept of the "highly qualified teacher" resulted in a tight labor market for special education teachers that were fully qualified. Boe notes that the NCLB defined the concept of a "highly qualified teacher" and prescribed that all public school teachers of core subject matter be highly qualified by the end of the 2005–2006 school year (as cited in DOE 2004b). As noted earlier, NCLB defined a highly qualified teacher as one with a) a bachelor's degree, b) full certification, and c) demonstrated expertise in the subject matter of each core subject taught. Boe (2006) defines "shortages" of teachers in terms of having an adequate supply of teachers to meet NCLB requirements:

> Thus, there is a federal statutory quality demand for teachers who attain all three qualifications. Since all teachers of core subjects are required to be highly qualified by NCLB, the size of the national quality demand (i.e., the demand for teachers with specific qualifications) for such teachers is the same as the quantity demand for

such teachers. To the extent that the supply of qualified teachers does not satisfy the quality demand, there is a shortage of qualified teachers. This shortage, in turn, creates a quantity demand for the number of additional qualified teachers needed to satisfy the shortage. (p. 139)

Boe (2006) compares labor market conditions for special education teachers to those of general education teachers and finds that it is comparatively more challenging to fill job vacancies for fully certified special education teachers:

> The magnitude of the chronic shortage of fully certified SETs [special education teachers] for students aged 6–21 years with disabilities can also be viewed by contrasting the shortage of SETs with that of GETs [general education teachers]. Available evidence suggests that for students in grades K–12, the shortage of fully certified GETs stood at 10.5% (based on the 1999/2000 SASS [Schools and Staffing Survey] data), whereas the comparable shortage of SETs stood at 13.7% (also based on 1999/2000 SASS data, adjusted upward by 1.1% to account for vacant positions). (p. 144)

Boe (2006) indicates that even if some reduction in demand for fully certified special education teachers is achieved, there is little reason to expect that the need for a much larger supply will be offset substantially in the future. He concludes that an increase in teacher supply is needed to address the chronic and increasing shortage of more than 50,000 fully certified special education teachers nationwide for students aged 6 to 21. He suggests four possible strategies to increase supply: 1) increased transfer of qualified general education teachers to teaching positions in special education, 2) improved recruitment of qualified teachers entering from the reserve pool, 3) expansion of initiatives to upgrade the qualifications of unqualified employed special education teachers, and 4) expansion of teacher preparation programs in special education to increase the production of novice teachers. He concludes that, of these strategies, upgrading the qualifications of employed special education teachers represents the most promising approach to increasing the supply of qualified teachers. He points out that such underqualified teachers are in abundance:

> Almost 50,000 employed SETs [special education teachers] nationally have not earned full certification in their main teaching assignment. However, they have demonstrated that they are

able and willing to be employed in special education. Therefore, these teachers can be viewed, for the most part, as an asset worthy of further investment in upgrading their qualifications. This can be implemented by local education agencies encouraging, supporting, and providing incentives for such teachers to complete alternative routes to certification (ARC) or to enroll part-time in traditional teacher preparation programs at local colleges and universities. (pp. 148–149)

RESPONSES TO LABOR MARKET CONDITIONS

This section examines some of the responses to tight labor market conditions for special education teachers, including responses that have been or could be undertaken by employers, the government, or special education teachers.

Use of Alternative Routes to Certification

Alternative routes to certification in special education tend to fast-track or circumvent traditional university-based teacher education. Alternative programs prepare teachers in nontraditional ways and allow individuals without traditional undergraduate teacher preparation to obtain teacher credentials. Alternative routes to certification in special education open doors to teaching for people who may not have otherwise pursued such a career. Teacher preparation programs tend to vary in length and structure, delivery mode, and target population. However, alternative programs tend to be shorter than traditional programs and are structured to allow candidates to begin teaching immediately or soon after beginning the program. In addition, alternative programs typically rely more heavily on field experiences than traditional preparation programs and less on formal classroom instruction. Compared to traditional certification, alternative program candidates are more likely to have majors unrelated to special education or general education teacher preparation (Rosenberg and Sindelar 2005). A typical alternative certification training program involves a summer course lasting six to eight weeks, followed by a paid supervised internship lasting up to one year, after which the teacher is expected to receive full certification.

The major concern regarding alternative certification programs is the impact that they may have on the quality of special education teaching. Critics claim that acceptance of such certification practices represents a reduction of teaching standards and will result in inadequately prepared teachers—and ultimately, ineffectively served children. Opponents charge that they create a two-tiered system of entry into teaching, one with negligible standards and the other with clear standards and rigorous assessments for those who choose traditional training. Advocates of such programs, on the other hand, argue that alternative certification requirements, when thoughtfully developed, will maintain the quality of teaching in special education and still allow talented candidates to enter the field with ease. Proponents of alternative certification view certification requirements as barriers to the recruitment of high-quality candidates and argue that alternate routes offer opportunities for candidates with strong subject matter knowledge or prior professional experience in other fields to improve the quality of the teaching force (Birkeland and Peske 2004).

Recent studies have found that most alternative education programs require baccalaureate degrees, have entrance requirements equal to or greater than those for university teacher education programs, emphasize practical training and experience over educational methods and training seminars, and involve ongoing supervision and evaluation of the candidates. Although critics cite the potential danger of producing lower quality teachers, approximately 50,000 individuals were issued teaching certificates through alternative routes in 2004–2005, up from approximately 39,000 the year before (Feistritzer 2006). As of 2005, there were 115 alternative routes to teacher certification being implemented by approximately 485 providers in 43 states and the District of Columbia, and more states are likely to consider such programs if the perceived shortage of special education teachers in certain critical-demand areas continues (Feistritzer 2005). For example, a study by Raymond, Fletcher, and Luque indicates that Teach for America (TFA) teachers are as competent as their non-TFA counterparts.[6] Employers use alternative certification programs for many reasons: they offer greater access to teaching for nontraditional candidates, they help provide teachers to underserved geographical areas, they attract candidates to subject areas of perpetual shortages, they draw in promising candidates who might otherwise pursue different careers, and they permit candidates to bypass extra hurdles faced in traditional programs (Nakai and Turley 2003).

Use of Uncertified Special Education Teachers

Table 2.7 shows, by state, the percentage of special education teachers that are not fully certified. During the fall of 2002, 12.4 percent (398,199) of the employed special education teachers were not fully certified, which translates to 12.4 percent or 730,716 students with special needs being taught by teachers who are not fully certified. This fell slightly in the fall of 2003 to 10.5 percent (361,458) of employed special education teachers being not fully certified, which was close to the 10 percent rate during the 1999–2000 school year. However, one-quarter of special education teachers during the 1999–2000 school year did not have an undergraduate or graduate major in special education (DOE 2002).

The data in Table 2.7 illustrate the large variation in certification rates among states. Although Connecticut is the only state that never had uncertified special education teachers in all the years covered, Iowa also employed only fully certified special education teachers in 2003. And in another 17 states, in the fall of 2003, special education teachers who were not fully certified made up 5 percent or less of the total number. At the other extreme, more than 20 percent of the special education teachers were not fully certified in seven states. In the District of Columbia, 30 percent of the special education teachers lacked full certification. Interestingly, the relationship between per capita income and the proportion lacking full certification is not strong. For example, in Alabama and Mississippi, less than 5 percent of the special education teachers lack full certification, while in the relatively wealthy states of California, New York, and Hawaii, well over 10 percent of the special education teachers lack full certification.

Several research studies have also shown that the school administrators have been meeting the demand for special education teachers by hiring teachers who are not fully certified. A study by Boe and Cooke (2006) found that the percentage of not-fully-certified special education teachers increased from 7.4 percent in 1993–1994 to 12.2 percent in 2001–2002. Over this time period, the shortage of fully certified special education teachers ranged from 2 to 4 percent higher each year than the shortage of fully certified general education teachers. In addition, the study found that the number of additional fully certified special education teachers needed almost doubled, from 25,000 in 1993–1994 to 49,000 in 2001–2002. This situation was further exacerbated by the qualifications of the teachers entering the profession, since only 44.4 percent of entering special education teachers were fully certified.

The inadequate supply of fully certified special education teachers is a major issue facing the field because many (over 10 percent, as shown above) special education teachers do not meet IDEA's "highly qualified" teacher requirement. According to the DOE, state education agencies must ensure that all special education teachers are highly qualified and that the local education agencies are taking measurable steps to recruit, train, hire, and retain highly qualified special education teachers. If local education agencies are failing to pursue these actions, the state must take measures appropriate to the situation to bring the local education agency into compliance with IDEA. The Office of Elementary and Secondary Education currently monitors the implementation of the highly qualified teacher standards. The Office of Special Education Programs collects data about special education personnel qualifications and requires states to establish and maintain qualifications to ensure that personnel are appropriately and adequately prepared and trained (DOE 2007).

However, states currently have the added flexibility of using their own separate High Objective Uniform State Standard of Evaluation (HOUSSE) standards for special education teachers under NCLB and IDEA, provided that any adaptations of the state's HOUSSE would not establish a lower standard for the content knowledge requirements for special education teachers and meets all the requirements of HOUSSE for regular education teachers (34 CFR 300.18[e]). Special education teachers hired before the 2002–2003 school year may demonstrate competence based on their state's HOUSSE. HOUSSE allows teachers to demonstrate knowledge without necessarily having to complete further training or testing. Some states use point systems for various professional development activities, peer and supervisor evaluations, and portfolios developed by teachers to meet HOUSSE requirements.

In addition, new teachers (those hired after July 1, 2002) may qualify under HOUSSE under two certain circumstances: 1) the alternative standards provision, where special educators who exclusively teach

Table 2.7 Percentage of Special Education Teachers Not Fully Certified for Students Aged 6–21, by State

State	1999–2000	2000–2001	Fall 2001	Fall 2002	Fall 2003
Alabama	3.4	2.6	3.1	3.3	3.4
Alaska	4.9	5.1	5.7	1.3	2.1
Arizona	7.7	10.9	13.2	15.1	13.9
Arkansas	5.5	9.9	5.7	5.9	7.0
California	22.6	23.6	24.4	23.1	19.2
Colorado	17.9	21.6	23.1	19.8	20.1
Connecticut	0.0	0.0	0.0	0.0	0.0
Delaware	22.3	31.8	30.9	25.2	15.5
District of Columbia	6.0	6.4	59.2	75.9	30.6
Florida	14.1	14.0	13.6	13.2	9.8
Georgia	3.1	3.7	21.9	25.9	22.0
Hawaii	22.8	27.6	20.2	25.7	22.5
Idaho	2.9	7.7	7.8	4.4	5.0
Illinois	4.5	5.5	6.5	3.8	3.3
Indiana	12.2	13.3	14.4	12.7	11.1
Iowa	11.8	11.4	10.0	6.3	0.0
Kansas	2.8	4.6	5.9	5.4	4.9
Kentucky	12.4	15.7	18.8	17.2	15.6
Louisiana	31.5	31.2	31.5	29.4	27.1
Maine	12.0	7.1	10.5	9.9	6.5
Maryland	11.6	13.9	18.1	18.1	20.6
Massachusetts	0.0	0.0	0.0	10.5	8.2

Michigan	6.1	8.2	10.0	12.4	10.5
Minnesota	7.6	9.0	7.8	7.8	5.2
Mississippi	7.7	8.3	10.0	1.9	1.2
Missouri	7.0	7.1	9.0	7.7	9.0
Montana	8.8	4.5	3.8	4.1	3.6
Nebraska	0.8	2.4	3.0	2.7	2.1
Nevada	3.6	2.9	12.6	15.1	15.7
New Hampshire	13.6	17.0	18.7	19.3	—
New Jersey	1.4	2.1	4.8	6.1	6.8
New Mexico	6.8	9.7	8.3	10.6	8.3
New York	19.7	25.2	20.5	21.1	15.5
North Carolina	14.5	17.3	18.3	19.3	16.7
North Dakota	6.1	5.0	5.3	3.9	4.6
Ohio	4.6	4.5	4.4	4.8	5.1
Oklahoma	1.2	1.7	2.3	2.4	1.7
Oregon	4.0	4.3	5.1	5.6	4.1
Pennsylvania	0.6	0.3	1.1	1.6	1.6
Rhode Island	1.2	2.1	6.1	9.4	3.9
South Carolina	8.2	7.1	8.4	9.6	6.3
South Dakota	2.2	2.4	4.0	5.9	9.9
Tennessee	1.5	1.6	1.4	1.1	6.4
Texas	13.7	11.1	11.4	12.1	14.2
Utah	12.5	6.1	8.0	6.6	6.7
Vermont	4.6	4.5	7.4	11.4	9.0

Table 2.7 (continued)

State	1999–2000	2000–2001	Fall 2001	Fall 2002	Fall 2003
Virginia	13.5	16.4	15.1	15.0	7.1
Washington	1.2	1.0	2.8	3.1	1.9
West Virginia	14.2	18.1	17.4	18.0	20.5
Wisconsin	2.8	2.3	3.4	3.0	1.5
Wyoming	5.1	4.6	6.8	4.7	7.7
Nationwide	10.0	11.5	12.2	12.4	10.5

NOTE: — = not submitted.
SOURCE: DOE (2002–2006).

students assessed by alternative standards have options for meeting the highly qualified mandate; and 2) new teachers in core content areas, where special educators who are highly qualified in math, language arts, or science have two years from the date of employment to qualify for the other subjects they teach using the HOUSSE requirements (Billingsley 2008).

Therefore, the use of special education teachers that are not highly qualified teachers as outlined under IDEA is generally not condoned, but there may be exceptions for uncertified teachers with state HOUSSE requirements if they meet one of three conditions: 1) fall under IDEA's category of "experienced" and were hired before the 2002–2003 school year, 2) teach students who are assessed by alternative standards, or 3) are highly qualified in at least one subject area. Perhaps the state flexibility of implementing HOUSSE for special educators allows school administrators to hire less than highly qualified teachers. The increased use of uncertified special education teachers indicates that there is an inadequate supply of highly qualified special education teachers, and in light of the regulations under IDEA and NCLB, this may indicate an overall shortage in the field, depending on the definition of "shortage" used.

Other Potential Approaches to Expanding Supply

Much of the research conducted by Boe and others cited above concludes that it is critical to increase the supply of highly qualified special education teachers. One approach, discussed above, is to increase the availability of alternative routes to certification. Another approach is to increase opportunities for individuals to prepare to become special education teachers by offering more generous financial aid to individuals who take courses in special education. This aid could take the form of scholarships or loan forgiveness for individuals who receive degrees in special education and practice in the field.

Employers who perceive a shortage of personnel may intensify their recruiting efforts or offer financial incentives to entice applicants. Some of the strategies employed by school districts in the past that could be used in the future to expand the supply of special education teachers (and reduce attrition) include offering the following types of financial incentives: signing bonuses, salary advances, assistance with acquiring homes (such as offering low down payments on homes, paying closing costs, and providing low-rate mortgages and counseling on home buying), paying for course work to earn certification in special education, student loan repayment, bonuses for teaching in critical demand areas or schools, and grants to cover professional development costs. Billingsley (2005) has also suggested several other possible strategies for improving working conditions that could potentially encourage entry or reduce attrition in the field of special education teaching. These include having a principal and staff who are knowledgeable about and interested in providing programs for students with disabilities, offering strong induction and mentoring programs and professional development opportunities, providing a reasonable teaching materials budget, job sharing, and reducing responsibilities during the first year.

CONCLUSIONS AND RECOMMENDATIONS

The labor market for special education teachers is particularly interesting because both the supply and demand sides are strongly affected by government actions at the federal, state, and local levels. At the federal level, laws such as NCLB and IDEA push states and local governments to use individuals who are deemed "highly qualified" by the legislation. Local school districts, however, have difficulty paying relatively high salaries for special education to increase retention because of financial pressure and institutional pressures to pay teachers similar salaries.

Using a strict economist's definition, the special education teacher labor market is, for the most part, not experiencing labor shortages at the time of our study. As Boe has pointed out in many of his studies, the vast majority of special education students do have a teacher in the classroom. The fact that a substantial minority of these teachers do not meet the criteria to be considered highly qualified is not surprising—it is a natural response by employers in any labor market where employers have difficulty filling positions to lower the standards for employees they hire.

Legislation such as IDEA and NCLB forces the nation to take note of the fact that children in special education are not all being taught by "highly qualified" instructors, but they do not guarantee that local school districts will hire only people who meet the requirements for being highly qualified. Contrast this situation to what would occur in a hospital that is having difficulty attracting physicians to perform surgery for patients. The hospital cannot substitute other personnel, such as nurses or veterinarians, to perform surgery, and some patients might have to be turned away.

Thus, the special education teacher labor market is far from a free market, and it is largely the actions of various government agencies that will determine how the labor market issues are resolved. The tight labor market, containing a substantial number of teachers deemed not to be highly qualified, signifies a possible "social demand shortage," as described in the first chapter. To resolve this situation, some additional research is needed and some difficult policy decisions are required. First, the public should decide how important it is to have "highly qualified" teachers in special education positions. Are the credentials required truly necessary or worth the cost of obtaining them? If so, perhaps the requirements for employing highly qualified special education teachers should be strengthened. If not, then the current situation where some special education positions are filled with individuals who do not meet all the requirements for being highly qualified may be adequate. Second, although there is not unanimity in the literature, much of the research indicates that retention could be improved in special education. Local school systems should be encouraged to explore approaches including pay differentials and ways of reducing stress on the job as means to improve retention and possibly attract new individuals to the field. Finally, to a large extent, salaries in special education are determined by government decisions rather than by private market forces. As many of the individuals we interviewed stated, higher salaries are likely to attract more individuals to the field, attract more able individuals, and reduce attrition. Special education teachers fill an important niche in the public education system, and we can anticipate that both quantity and quality problems will be reduced somewhat if salaries are increased.

Notes

1. As might be expected, dual certification has important consequences for the supply of special education teachers. First, it extends the investment in time and training required for special education certification, and second, it influences special education teachers' possible career paths, allowing them to enter general education easily and immediately. The relevance of these two factors to labor shortages in the occupation is discussed later.

2. States currently have the added flexibility of using their own separate High Objective Uniform State Standard of Evaluation (HOUSSE) standards for special education teachers under NCLB and IDEA, provided that any adaptations of the state's HOUSSE would not establish a lower standard for the content knowledge requirements for special education teachers and meet all the requirements of a HOUSSE for regular education teachers (34 CFR 300.18[e]). Additional discussion with regard to HOUSSE appears later in this chapter.

3. For example, SpecialNet, a nationwide computer network developed by GTE and the National Association of State Directors of Special Education, has an employment bulletin board that lists employment opportunities nationwide. Another electronic service is CAREER CONNECTION, which lists candidates seeking special education positions. Several state agencies have also developed such systems to rapidly and effectively disseminate teacher vacancy information.

4. Universities generally design their teacher education curricula around their state's certification requirements; consequently, the requirements of in-state employers generally match university curricula, and new teachers find it easiest to obtain jobs in the state in which they were educated.

5. Many of those who receive temporary or emergency certification are general education teachers who are simply reassigned within the same school district; thus, the need for a job search is often unnecessary.

6. Cited in Birkeland and Peske (2004).

3
Pharmacists

We selected pharmacists for a case study because there have been many reports in the popular and academic literature about shortages in the field, including a congressionally mandated study in 2000 (DHHS 2000). The labor market for this profession is interesting for several reasons. Many health care professions are facing the strains of increased demand, but the market demand for pharmacists is related to the increase in demand for prescription drugs in particular. There are a variety of other factors to explore in understanding the market conditions for pharmacists, including the recent shift in education requirements, the expanding role of pharmacists (e.g., in consultation with patients and physicians), the increase in pharmacy services available at grocery stores and other locations, the use of pharmacist technicians and aides as a labor substitute to perform some duties formerly performed by pharmacists, an increase in the use of automation in processing prescriptions, and the rise of third-party payers for prescriptions.

BACKGROUND AND DESCRIPTION

The primary duty of pharmacists is the distribution of prescription drugs to individuals. However, pharmacists have several other responsibilities, including advising patients on the selections, dosages, interactions, and side effects of medications, as well as monitoring the health and progress of patients to ensure the proper use of medication. Very few pharmacists spend much time compounding (doing the actual mixing of ingredients to form medications) because most medications are now produced by pharmaceutical companies in standard dosages that are delivery-ready. A majority of pharmacists work in community settings—retail drugstores or health care facilities such as hospitals, nursing homes, and mental health institutions. Increasingly, pharmacists are pursuing nontraditional roles and careers, including conducting research or marketing for pharmaceutical manufacturers, developing benefit packages or performing cost-benefit analyses for health insurance companies, and teaching at colleges and universities. In addition, some pharmacists work for government agencies, public health care service organizations, and pharmacy associations (BLS 2010b).

Pharmacists in community settings dispense medications, counsel patients on the use of medications, and advise physicians about patients' medication therapy. Community pharmacists also provide patients with information on general health topics, such as diet and exercise, and over-the-counter medications and other medical products. In addition, pharmacists have a great deal of paperwork to fill out, including third-party insurance forms. Pharmacists who own or manage a community pharmacy may have additional duties, such as selling other merchandise, overseeing personnel, and managing the general operations of the pharmacy. Some community pharmacies also provide specialized services to help patients with specific conditions, such as diabetes, asthma, smoking cessation, and high blood pressure. Some pharmacists are also authorized to administer vaccinations to their patients (BLS 2010b).

Pharmacists in health care facilities dispense medications and advise medical staff on the selection and effects of prescription drugs. These pharmacists may also make sterile solutions to be administered intravenously to patients. In addition, health care pharmacists plan, monitor, and evaluate patient drug programs. Pharmacists working in home health care monitor drug therapy and prepare medications for use in the home, such as infusions, which are solutions prepared for patient injection. Some pharmacists specialize in specific drug therapy areas, such as intravenous nutrition support, oncology, nuclear pharmacy, geriatric pharmacy, and psychiatric pharmacy (BLS 2010b).

Pharmacy technicians and pharmacy aides often assist in performing several of pharmacists' responsibilities. Pharmacy technicians help licensed pharmacists provide medication and other health care products to patients. Technicians tend to perform routine tasks to help prepare prescribed medication, such as counting tablets and labeling prescriptions. Pharmacy technicians also perform administrative duties, such as answering phones, stocking shelves, and operating cash registers. Pharmacy technicians in community pharmacies have varying responsibilities, depending on state rules and regulations. For example, some states allow technicians to prepare prescriptions, which must be checked by a pharmacist before being given to a patient. In addition, technicians may establish and maintain patient profiles, prepare insurance claim forms, and stock prescription and over-the-counter medications. In health-system pharmacies, technicians may have added responsibilities, including reading patients' charts and preparing appropriate medications, which may be delivered to the patient after pharmacist approval (BLS 2010b).

Pharmacy aides work closely with pharmacy technicians and perform a variety of administrative duties, including answering telephones, stocking shelves, and performing clerical duties. In addition, aides may establish and maintain patient profiles and prepare insurance claim forms. Pharmacy aides and technicians refer any questions regarding prescriptions and drug information to a pharmacist (BLS 2010b).

Both state and federal law regulate the pharmaceutical industry. Federal rules primarily address prescription drugs, while state rules tend to regulate pharmacists and pharmacist practice settings. In 1906, federal regulation of drugs began with the passage of the Pure Food and Drug Act, which required that labeling on medications be truthful. In 1914, the Harrison Narcotic Act was passed, which created the need for prescriptions for products exceeding the allowable limit of narcotics. In addition, this Act mandated increased record-keeping for physicians and pharmacists who dispense narcotic prescription drugs. In 1938, the Food, Drug, and Cosmetic Act (FDC) was passed, which required that new drugs be proven to be safe prior to marketing (DHHS 2008c).

There have been several subsequent amendments to the FDC Act. In 1951, the Durham-Humphrey Amendment was passed, which defines the kinds of drugs that cannot be used safely without medical supervision and restricts their sale to a prescription by a licensed practitioner. The 1961 Kefauver-Harris Drug Amendments required drug manufacturers to prove the effectiveness of their products to the FDA before marketing them. In 1983, the Orphan Drug Act passed, enabling the FDA to promote research and marketing of drugs needed for treating rare diseases, and the first televised drug commercial aired in June of that year. The 1984 Drug Price Competition and Patent Term Restoration Act both made marketing of generic equivalents of drugs easier and granted patent term extension to the innovators of new drugs, under certain conditions. In 1988, the Prescription Drug Marketing Act banned the diversion of prescription drugs from legitimate commercial channels. The Food and Drug Administration Modernization Act of

1997 clarified pharmacist responsibilities in drug distribution (DHHS 2008c).

More recently, final guidance was provided for pharmaceutical marketing in 1999, the Drug Safety Board was created in 2005, and the final regulation covering "Requirements on Content and Format of Labeling for Human Prescription Drug and Biological Products" was passed in 2006, including new content and format requirements for FDA-approved labeling (DHHS 2008c). On December 8, 2003, President Bush signed into law the Medicare Prescription Drug Improvement and Modernization Act (MMA) of 2003 (PL 108-173). MMA established a voluntary outpatient prescription drug benefit for people on Medicare, known as Part D, which went into effect January 1, 2006 (DHHS 2008a,b).

Overall, federal rules and regulations have created incentives for the pharmaceutical industry to produce more drugs, including allowing direct marketing of prescription drugs and encouraging the development of generic equivalents, thus increasing the need for pharmacists to dispense medications. In addition, federal rules and regulations created the classification of prescription drugs and outlined the requirements for dispensing drugs that exceed the specified narcotic level. These federal regulations add to the administrative burden of pharmacists, including record-keeping and labeling requirements.

State pharmacy boards are responsible for setting regulations, standards, and parameters within the pharmacy practice in each state. The three primary standards set by state pharmacy boards ensure that pharmacists check the patient's history, review current medications, and interact with the patient directly. A majority of the other standards address the dispensing of drugs, such as specific forms required for strict-access drugs and the confidentiality of patient information. Pharmacy board standards are developed in cooperation with pharmacy professionals, state legislatures, and consumer groups (Giorgianni 2002). The National Association of Boards of Pharmacy publishes the Model State Pharmacy Act and Model Rules of the National Association of Boards of Pharmacy (Model Act), which provide the boards of pharmacy with model language that may be used when developing state laws or board rules (National Association of Boards of Pharmacy 2007).

TRAINING AND RECRUITMENT OF WORKERS

This section discusses the educational requirements and qualifications to be a pharmacist, the factors affecting those requirements, and methods employers use to fill vacancies. This examination of the means by which individuals enter the occupation lays the groundwork for the analysis presented later in the chapter.

Educational Qualifications and Entry Requirements

Licensure of pharmacists is required in all states. Pharmacists must earn a Doctor of Pharmacy (PharmD) degree from a college of pharmacy to obtain a license. The PharmD degree has recently replaced the Bachelor of Pharmacy degree, which is no longer being awarded by colleges of pharmacy in the United States. The PharmD requires five years of postsecondary education, compared to the Bachelor of Pharmacy, which required four years of undergraduate education. PharmD applicants must have completed at least two years of postsecondary study with coursework in mathematics, natural sciences, humanities, and social sciences to be admitted to a PharmD program. A majority (70 percent) of the PharmD programs also require applicants to take the Pharmacy College Admissions Test, or PCAT (BLS 2010b).

The PharmD program is designed to teach students about all aspects of drug therapy, including communication with patients and other health care providers about drug information and patient care. In addition, students learn professional ethics, concepts of public health, and medication distribution systems management. Besides classroom instruction, students in PharmD programs spend about one-quarter of their time in a variety of pharmacy practice settings under the supervision of licensed pharmacists to gain hands-on experience (BLS 2010b).

In the 2006–2007 school year, 70 colleges of pharmacy also awarded a Master of Science (MS) or a Doctor of Philosophy (PhD) degree. In the 2009–2010 school year, in addition to the 11,487 PharmD degrees awarded, 773 MS and 450 PhD degrees were awarded (American Association of Colleges of Pharmacy 2011). Both the MS and PhD degrees are awarded after the completion of the PharmD program and are designed for those who want additional clinical, laboratory, and research experience. Areas of graduate study include pharmaceutical chemistry, the study of the physical and chemical properties of drugs and dosage forms; pharmacology, the study of the effects of drugs on the body; and pharmacy administration. Many pharmacists who earn an MS and a PhD degree go on to do research for pharmaceutical companies or teach at universities (BLS 2010b).

PharmD graduates who wish to gain further training also have the option of pursuing a one- or two-year residency or fellowship. Pharmacy residency programs, which are often required to become a hospital pharmacist, consist of postgraduate training in pharmacy practice and usually require the completion of a research project. Pharmacy fellowship programs are much more individualized and usually prepare participants to work in a specialized area of pharmacy, such as clinical practice or research laboratories (BLS 2010b).

In addition to requiring pharmacists to earn a PharmD, all states stipulate that pharmacists must pass the North American Pharmacists Licensure Exam (NAPLEX), which tests pharmacy skills and knowledge. Forty-four states and the District of Columbia also require the Multistate Pharmacy Jurisprudence Exam (MPJE), which tests knowledge of pharmacy law. Both of these exams are administered by the National Association of Boards of Pharmacy (NABP). The states that do not require passage of the MPJE require passage of their own state pharmacy law exams for licensure. As with many professions, some states have additional exams required that are unique to their jurisdiction. Currently, all states except California grant license transfers to qualified pharmacists who are already licensed in another jurisdiction. Most jurisdictions require continuing education for license renewal (BLS 2010b).

Most pharmacy technicians are trained on the job, but employers may prefer applicants that have formal training, certification, or previous experience. Formal education programs are offered by the military, some hospitals, vocational and technical colleges, and community colleges. Formal education programs require classroom and laboratory work in a variety of areas, including medical and pharmaceutical terminology, pharmaceutical calculations, pharmacy record keeping, pharmaceutical techniques, and pharmacy law and ethics. Many training programs include internships that give students an opportunity to gain hands-on experience in actual pharmacies. After completion of formal education programs, students receive a diploma certificate or associate's degree, depending on the program.

The Pharmacy Technician Certification Board and the Institute for the Certification of Pharmacy Technicians administer national certification exams, which are usually voluntary, but certification is required by some states and employers. Both exams require candidates to have a high school diploma or GED, no felony convictions in the past five years, and no drug- or pharmacy-related felony convictions at any time. Under both programs, technicians must be recertified every two years, which requires 20 hours of continuing education with at least one hour in pharmacy law (BLS 2010b). Pharmacy aides, on the other hand, are trained informally on the job, but employers favor applicants with at least a high school diploma. Many pharmacy aides become certified or undergo on-the-job training to become pharmacy technicians (BLS 2010b).

Methods Employers Use to Recruit Workers and Workers Use to Obtain Employment

Employers, such as chain drugstores and medical facility pharmacies, recruit new pharmacists through interactions with pharmacy training programs (e.g., PharmD programs) at universities and professional conferences or by placing advertisements in professional publications and on Web sites. Word of mouth also plays a role in the recruitment of new pharmacists entering the field, as well as in the recruiting of pharmacists already working at other pharmacies but looking to change jobs. Increasingly, employers utilize their own Web sites to advertise job openings, as well as advertising job openings on various health care or general employment Web sites.[1] For example, company Web sites, such as those for large chain drugstores run by Target and CVS, make it very easy for new and existing pharmacists to search for pharmacist jobs by locality or to contact a pharmacists' recruiter that covers a specific geographic area. A search on the Target Stores Web site produces a listing of openings such as the following (each job listing can be clicked on to provide additional information about the vacancy):

2010 D348 Pharmacy Intern Full-Time
United States
Job Posting: May 24, 2010—Requisition ID PHA00018B

2010 Pharmacy Exec in Training Full-Time
United States—Texas, United States—New Mexico,
United States—Oklahoma
Job Posting: Jan 29, 2010—Requisition ID PHA0000OM

D353 Pharmacy EIT 2010 Full-Time
United States—Louisiana
Job Posting: Apr 16, 2010—Requisition ID PHA00014A

These Web sites also make it very easy for candidates to apply for job vacancies and to contact job recruiters. Additionally, pharmacist associations have set up electronic bulletin boards to list vacancies available for pharmacist positions.[2]

The methods that pharmacists use to seek and obtain positions are generally similar to the methods employers use for recruitment. Pharmacists use university postings, word of mouth, employer Web sites, and a variety of employment Web sites to locate and apply for pharmacist openings. The following advice from a Web site provides step-by-step instructions for new entrants to the field of pharmacy, illustrating the various methods employers use to find qualified pharmacists and the ways in which newly trained pharmacists should go about finding a vacant position:[3]

- Step 1: Get job placement assistance from the careers office at your pharmacy school. This office will have contacts you can use to find current pharmacist openings in the areas of the country where you would most like to work.

- Step 2: Complete an internship. Most pharmacy schools require this as part of the program. The pharmacist for whom you intern may be able to refer you to places that are hiring or may even hire you once you've graduated.

- Step 3: Conduct a targeted resume blitz. Determine the places where you would most like to work, and then send out your resumes to each of them. Include your pharmacy school transcripts and a cover letter introducing yourself and highlighting some of your academic achievements.

- Step 4: Join a professional organization. Most states have professional pharmacist alliances. Become a member and attend group functions. You can make contacts at these events that could lead to a job down the road.

- Step 5: Visit a job board online, such as HealthCareRecruitment .com. Sites such as this have current listings for pharmacist jobs all across the United States.

EMPLOYMENT AND EARNINGS TRENDS

Employment Trends

Employment levels and change

As Table 3.1 shows, slightly less than half of all pharmacists (44.0 percent) work in health and personal care stores. The second-largest setting for pharmacists is hospitals, including general medical and surgical hospitals, where about one-fifth of pharmacists work. Pharmacists are less commonly employed in grocery stores (8.4 percent), department stores (6.6 percent), and other general merchandise stores (5.2 percent).

The number of pharmacists employed has steadily risen in the past decade (Table 3.2). The number of pharmacists increased every year

Table 3.1 Pharmacist Employment by Industry, 2010

Industry	Employment	%
Health and personal care stores	117,850	44.0
General medical and surgical hospitals	58,680	21.9
Grocery stores	22,520	8.4
Department stores	17,620	6.6
Other general merchandise stores	14,010	5.2
Other	37,350	13.9
Total	268,030	100.0

NOTE: Excludes self-employed persons.
SOURCE: BLS (2010b).

Table 3.2 Number and Percentage Change of Pharmacists and Other Health Care Occupations, 2006–2010

Occupation	2006	2007	2008	2009	2010	% change
Pharmacists	239,920	253,110	266,410	267,860	268,030	11.7
Pharmacy technicians	282,450	301,950	324,110	331,890	333,500	18.1
Pharmacy aides	47,810	49,630	53,190	52,230	49,580	3.7
Optometrists	24,220	24,900	25,970	26,480	26,480	9.3
Registered nurses	2,417,150	2,468,340	2,542,760	2,583,770	2,655,020	9.8
All health care practitioners and technical occupations	6,713,780	6,877,680	7,076,800	7,200,950	7,346,580	9.4
All workers from all occupations	132,604,980	134,354,250	135,185,230	130,647,610	127,097,160	−4.2

SOURCE: 2006–2009 data: BLS (2011a); 2010 data: BLS (2011b).

from 2006 to 2010, rising by a total of 11.7 percent, which is higher than the percentage increase for all health care practitioners (9.4 percent) over the same time period. Most notably, the employment numbers for all workers in all occupations decreased by 4.2 percent over the same period (with precipitous decreases in employment levels occurring from 2008 to 2010). Among the occupations compared in Table 3.2, only pharmacy technicians had a higher employment growth rate (18.1 percent) than pharmacists from 2006 to 2010.

The dramatic increase in pharmacy technicians over the past five years most likely reflects employers' hiring more pharmacy technicians to assist pharmacists with day-to-day tasks that do not have to be performed by a licensed pharmacist, such as preparing medications, answering phones, and completing third-party-payer paperwork. In contrast to pharmacy technicians, the percentage increase in employment of pharmacy aides (3.7 percent) lagged substantially and was well below the increase for all health care practitioners and technical occupations (9.4 percent). Pharmacy aides may have experienced less growth in employment than pharmacists and pharmacy technicians because of attrition and the expansion of pharmacy technicians' duties. The overall robust employment growth of pharmacists and pharmacy technicians over the five-year period (particularly in comparison to general trends for all workers) is an indicator of strong continuing demand for pharmacists and pharmacy technicians and is conducive to a tight labor market for these two occupations.

Unemployment trends

Another key indicator of labor market tightness and possible shortages is the annual average unemployment rate by occupation. Occupations experiencing tight labor markets, in which the number of vacancies is greater than the number of qualified applicants, are likely to have very low unemployment rates because those searching for jobs find them quickly and are unemployed for very short periods (Cohen 1990). Figure 3.1 illustrates the trend in the annual unemployment rate for pharmacists and other occupations. The annual unemployment rate for pharmacists averaged 1.6 percent between 2006 and 2010, compared to 1.8 percent for all health care practitioners and 6.2 percent for all workers from all occupations. Over the past five years, the unem-

Figure 3.1   Average Annual Unemployment Rate for Pharmacists, Other Health Care Occupations, and All Workers, 2006–2010

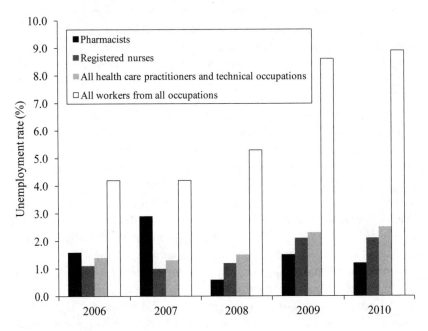

ployment rate for pharmacists has fluctuated from a low of 0.6 percent in 2008 to a high of 2.9 percent in 2007, well below the rate for all workers, although sometimes slightly above or below that for all health care practitioners. The unemployment rate for pharmacists—like that of nurses and other health care practitioners—is relatively low and conducive to a tight labor market.

Vacancy rates

The American Society of Health-System Pharmacists (ASHP) is a national professional association that represents pharmacists who practice in hospitals, health maintenance organizations, long-term care facilities, home care, and other components of health care systems and conducts an annual staffing survey to gauge the supply and demand of pharmacists. The pharmacist vacancy rate averaged 5.0 percent from 2006 to 2010, and that of pharmacy technicians was 4.1 percent over the same period (Figure 3.2). The rate was particularly high for pharmacists during the first three years of the period (in excess of 6 percent), well above the rate for pharmacy technicians. However, in 2009 and 2010, the vacancy rate for pharmacists dipped to a level just slightly below that of pharmacy technicians.

According to the ASHP staffing survey of 597 pharmacy directors, the average length of time required to fill a vacant position in 2006 was about six months (Scheckelhoff 2006). The relatively high vacancy rates (though gradually declining over the five-year period) and the sluggish rate at which employers are able to fill positions are indicative of possible tight labor market conditions for pharmacists, particularly from 2006 through 2008.

Pharmacies have also faced difficulties in filling vacancies for leadership positions. In 2005, 46 percent of employers recruiting for health-system management and leadership positions in pharmacies indicated that it took 3 to 6 months and 26 percent indicated it took 7 to 12 months

Figure 3.2 Vacancy Rates for Full-Time Equivalent Pharmacists and Pharmacy Technicians, 2007–2010

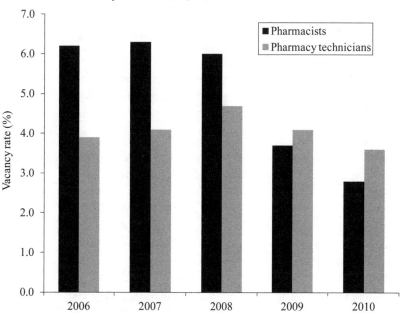

SOURCE: ASHP Pharmacy Staffing Survey Results (2009, 2010).

to fill these vacancies. More than half the employers indicated that recruiting was more difficult than it had been three years ago, and 40 percent indicated it was about the same. Factors contributing to the difficulties in hiring pharmacists for leadership positions included lack of pharmacists with leadership or management experience (55 percent), lack of interest among current pharmacists (50 percent), and suboptimal salaries (50 percent) (White 2005).

Projections for future employment growth within the occupation

Employment growth for pharmacists has been rapid during the past five years (Table 3.2), and continued growth is anticipated in the future, as shown in Table 3.3. The BLS estimates that the total number of pharmacists will increase by 17 percent from 2008 to 2018, compared to an estimated 31 percent increase for pharmacy technicians and 6 percent decrease for pharmacy aides over the same period. The increase in pharmacist employment is expected to greatly exceed the increase for all workers in all occupations, which is estimated at about 10 percent for this time period.

Earnings Trends

The relative wage rate change in an occupation is often an important indicator of labor market dynamics, especially in the short run. In occupations where market forces move freely, a rapid rise in wages may indicate the presence of a shortage. This appears to be true in the case

Table 3.3 Employment for Pharmacists, Other Health Care Occupations, and All Workers, 2008 and 2018 (projected)

Occupation	2008	Projected 2018	% change
Pharmacists	270,000	316,000	17.0
Pharmacy technicians	326,000	426,000	30.6
Pharmacy aides	55,000	52,000	−6.3
Optometrists	35,000	43,000	24.4
Registered nurses	2,619,000	3,200,000	22.0
All workers from all occupations	150,931,000	166,206,000	10.1

SOURCE: BLS (2010b).

of pharmacists, at least until recently, as they have seen a substantial increase in median hourly earnings compared to all health care practitioners and also compared to workers from all occupations, as shown in Table 3.4. Pharmacists' wages have consistently increased over the past five years, rising 18.0 percent overall for the period, from $45.44 in 2006 to $53.64 in 2010. This compares to an 11.4 percent increase in median earnings for all workers over the same period. Pharmacy technicians also experienced an increase in wages: their pay rose 10.8 percent for the period, from $12.32 in 2006 to $13.65 in 2010. Because the labor market for pharmacists has been largely determined by market forces, the higher-than-average increase in median earnings for pharmacists since 2006 is indicative of a tight labor market, as employers have increased wage levels to remain competitive in recruiting new pharmacists and in holding onto the ones they already have.

LABOR MARKET FACTORS CONTRIBUTING TO A SHORTAGE

This section assesses the most prominent factors on the demand and supply sides that affect labor market conditions for pharmacists. The

Table 3.4 Median Hourly Earnings ($) and Percentage Change for Pharmacists, Comparison Occupations, and All Workers, 2006–2010

Occupation	2006	2007	2008	2009	2010	% change
Pharmacists	45.44	48.31	51.16	52.49	53.64	18.0
Pharmacy technicians	12.32	12.85	13.32	13.49	13.65	10.8
Pharmacy aides	9.35	9.39	9.66	10.00	10.31	10.3
Optometrists	43.77	26.17	46.31	46.22	45.67	4.3
Registered nurses	27.54	28.85	30.03	30.65	31.10	12.9
All health care practitioners and technical occupations	24.99	26.17	27.20	27.74	28.12	12.5
All workers from all occupations	14.61	15.10	15.57	15.95	16.27	11.4

SOURCE: BLS (2011c).

factors discussed have been singled out in the literature on pharmacists and in interviews conducted as part of this study with individuals from associations and academia knowledgeable about pharmacist trends.

Demand-Side Factors

Increased use of prescription drugs

In 2006, the U.S. pharmacy industry had more than $216 billion in sales and dispensed over 3.4 billion prescriptions. In 2006, retail pharmacies filled more than 2.4 billion prescriptions, with the average person filling five written prescriptions every year (National Association of Chain Drug Stores 2007). Spending on prescription drugs in the United States reached $249.9 billion by 2009—more than six times the $40.3 billion spent in 1990. The share of prescription drug costs paid by private health insurance has also increased in recent years, from 26 percent in 1990 to 44 percent in 2006. With the implementation of the Medicare Part D prescription drug benefit, the government's share rose from 28 percent in 2005 to 34 percent in 2006. These increases in the share paid by both government and private insurance contributed to a decline in the amount of out-of-pocket expenses consumers paid for prescription drugs: their share of the costs dropped from 56 percent in 1990 to 22 percent in 2006 (Kaiser Family Foundation 2008). Several interviewees pointed to the rapid growth in the number of prescription drugs as the driving factor in the increased demand for pharmacists. For example, according to one interviewee, the push for more pharmacists to fill prescriptions has been closely linked to rapid increases in prescriptions:

> Between 1998 and 2008, there was about a 50 percent increase in prescriptions filled. There are a number of factors that have driven this increase, but the most important has been the increased third-party coverage of prescription drugs through the Medicare Part D and private insurance. For example, in 1990 cash (self-pay) prescriptions accounted for about two-thirds (63.1 percent) of all prescriptions; by 2008, only about a tenth (10.8 percent) of prescriptions were self-pay. The aging of the population and direct-to-consumer advertising has also been a factor—but the big driver has been the increasing reliance on third-party payments, which means the payment is not coming out of the patient's pocket.

As shown in Figure 3.3, national expenditures on prescription drugs have increased dramatically, from $77.6 billion in 1997 to $249.9 billion in 2009. From 2005 to 2009, spending on prescription drugs in the United States jumped by more than 25 percent. Expenditures increased every year during that period, with a 9 percent increase from 2005 to 2006 alone (DHHS 2007a). In addition, the DHHS forecasts that prescription drug spending will increase from $249.9 billion in 2009 to $457.8 billion in 2019, almost doubling during the 10-year period.

Aging of the population and Medicare

The population aged 65 years or older has grown substantially in recent years. In 2009, there were 39.6 million elderly people (12.9 percent of the total U.S. population), which is a 15.1 percent increase from 1998, when there were 34.4 million elderly Americans. The total population of older Americans is expected to increase to 72.1 million in 2030 (DHHS 2010).

Figure 3.3 Prescription Drug Expenditure Trends, 1997–2009

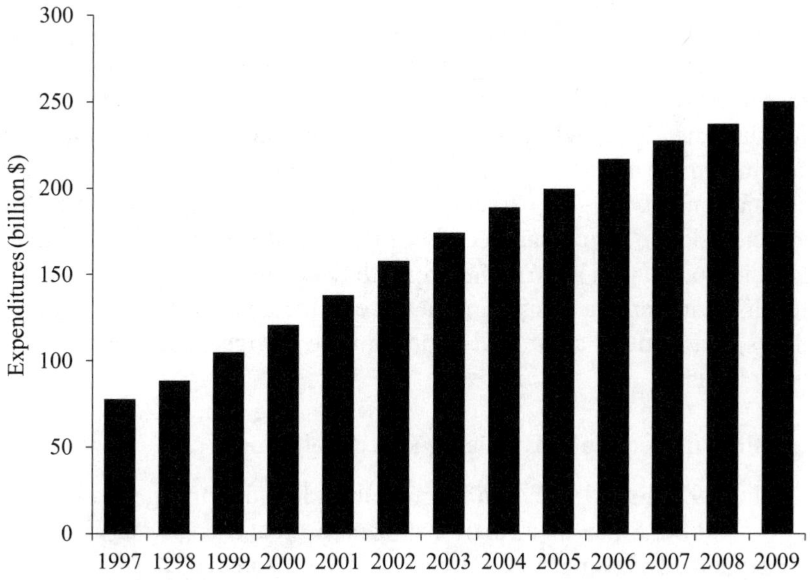

SOURCE: U.S. DHHS (2008b).

The growth in the proportion of older Americans in the population is a significant factor in the need for pharmacists because older people tend to spend more on health care and drug prescriptions. In 2009, older consumers averaged $4,846 in out-of-pocket health care expenditures, a 61 percent increase from 1999. In contrast, the total population spent considerably less, averaging $3,126 in out-of-pocket costs. About 17 percent of older Americans' out-of-pocket health care expenditures were on prescription drugs, as older Americans spent an average of $828 on prescription drugs in 2009. Medicare is the public insurance program for Americans over the age of 65, and in 2009, almost all (93.5 percent) noninstitutionalized persons aged 65 and over were covered by Medicare (DHHS 2010). Since 2006, when the new Medicare Part D prescription drug benefit went into effect, Medicare beneficiaries have had access to prescription drug coverage offered by private plans, either stand-alone prescription drug plans or Medicare Advantage prescription drug plans. Medicare drug plans receive payments from the government to provide Medicare-subsidized drug coverage to enrolled beneficiaries. As of 2009, more than 26 million Medicare beneficiaries were enrolled in Medicare drug plans, including 17.5 million in stand-alone prescription drug plans and 9 million in Medicare Advantage plans (Kaiser Family Foundation 2009).

According to a 2006 survey of 802 pharmacists, 53 percent of the respondents found the administrative burden of filling prescriptions for customers covered by the new Medicare drug plans worse than the administrative burden under typical commercial insurance plans. In addition, nearly all (97 percent) of the pharmacists surveyed had customers ask for help or advice about the Medicare drug plans (Kaiser Family Foundation 2006). Therefore, the new prescription drug benefit results in not only a significant increase in the demand for prescription drugs, but also for additional counseling to navigate the new government benefit.

Pharmaceutical advertising and development

In 1997, the FDA revised its guidelines for advertising medications to the public. Since then, there has been a great increase in direct-to-consumer advertising: 2009 spending was estimated at $4.3 billion, over twice the $1.8 billion spent in 1999. Although a majority of advertising continues to be directed toward physicians, spending directed at physicians decreased from $6.8 billion in 2008 to $6.6 billion in 2009 (Kaiser Family Foundation 2010a). The increase in direct advertising has led to consumers asking for specific prescription drugs by name after seeing a commercial on television or hearing an advertisement on the radio. This has resulted in a relatively new source of demand by consumers actively seeking prescription drugs, as opposed to patients who wait for doctors to prescribe medications. Two study interviewees identified direct-to-consumer advertising as a factor behind increased demand for prescription drugs (thereby increasing demand for pharmacists). For example, one interviewee stated, "In recent years, direct-to-consumer advertising by pharmaceutical companies has increased demand for medication and pressures on doctors to prescribe."

Increased use and availability of over-the-counter drugs and expansion in the number of pharmacies and hours of operation

The number of over-the-counter drugs has grown significantly—in 2000, there were more than 100,000 over-the-counter drugs available, and more than 600 of these contained ingredients and dosages available only by prescription 20 years earlier. The increased availability of over-the-counter drugs reclassified from prescription status offers consumers more choices and greater flexibility. However, this greater selection results in the need for pharmacists to provide more counseling to consumers (DHHS 2000). With the increase in demand for both over-the-counter and prescription drugs, there has been an increase in the number of pharmacies, and many pharmacies have expanded their hours. For example, according to one study interviewee, "Competition among chain stores has led to increases in hours—creating a demand for pharmacists. There has also been expansion in settings for pharmacies in venues such as grocery stores and discount stores, resulting in increased demand." Since state pharmacy laws require a pharmacist on site when prescription medications are dispensed, new store openings and expanded hours increased pressure to hire and employ more pharmacists (DHHS 2000).

The increased demand for prescription drugs also results in the need for more of a pharmacist's time to be devoted to filling prescriptions, filling out paperwork for third-party payers, and other administrative tasks. However, according to a 2004 survey of pharmacists who were asked about their time spent in various work activities, pharmacists would like to devote more of their time to consultation and drug-use management activities in community pharmacy settings (Schommer et al. 2005). In addition, the change in education requirements with the shift to PharmD has changed the type, competencies, and practice expectations of pharmacy graduates. As a result, PharmD graduates have expanded opportunities, and there has been an increased demand for these graduates in nontraditional environments, including pharmaceutical and clinical research in the business sector involving activities such as insurance, managed care, and benefits management (Cohen et al. 2001).

Supply-Side Factors

Longer training period

Until 2004, two degree programs, the BS in pharmacy and the PharmD, were offered for accreditation by the American Council of Pharmaceutical Education (ACPE). The BS has gradually been phased out throughout the United States, and the ACPE only accredited PharmD programs after 2003. The PharmD program was first introduced in 1992, when the House of Delegates of the American Association of Colleges of Pharmacy adopted it as the entry-level degree after much consideration and debate. During the conversion process, the number of graduates was lower because of the extra year required in the PharmD program as compared to the BS. A majority of schools transitioned to the new degree program gradually, so the impact on graduate numbers was spread out over time; however, some schools began the PharmD for an entire class in a single year, so there were no graduates one year. Several responses to a request for comments in the *Federal Register* in 2000 noted that employers experienced difficulties because of reduced numbers of graduates during the transition to the PharmD program (DHHS 2000). One study interviewee noted that the switch to the PharmD degree created a temporary but noticeable tightness in the labor market for pharmacists:

> Demand for pharmacists (and shortage conditions) peaked in about 1999–2000. At that time, the National Association of Chain

Drug Stores (NACDS) had a lot of members complaining that they could not fill positions. Tight labor market conditions were closely associated with regulatory change, which switched pharmacists' training from a bachelor's degree to a 5-year doctoral (PharmD) degree. This change added one additional year of training, a one-year practicum. This practicum replaced time that previously had been spent working under the supervision of a pharmacist. The result was that one whole year of work among those training to become pharmacists was pulled out of the labor market.

As of July 2011, 119 U.S. colleges and schools of pharmacy had accredited professional degree programs. In the fall of 2010, first professional degree enrollment in these institutions ranged from 62 to 1,833 students (up from 45 to 1,754 students in 2008), with an average applicant-to-enrollment rate of 7.7:1 (American Association of Colleges of Pharmacy 2011). As Table 3.5 shows, the number of pharmacy graduates was affected during the transition to the PharmD program. Although the PharmD program was first introduced in 1992, a majority

Table 3.5   The Shift to PharmD as the First Professional Degree Obtained, 1997–2010

Year	BS pharmacy Graduates	%	PharmD Graduates	%	Total first professional
1997	5,768	74.2	2,004	25.8	7,772
1998	4,768	64.4	2,632	35.6	7,400
1999	3,876	54.3	3,265	45.7	7,141
2000	2,956	40.7	4,304	59.3	7,260
2001	1,914	27.3	5,086	72.7	7,000
2002	1,415	18.7	6,158	81.3	7,573
2003	839	11.2	6,649	88.8	7,488
2004	388	4.8	7,770	95.2	8,158
2005	26	0.3	8,242	99.7	8,268
2006	—	0.0	9,040	100.0	9,040
2007	—	0.0	9,812	100.0	9,812
2008	—	0.0	10,500	100.0	10,500
2009	—	0.0	10,988	100.0	10,988
2010	—	0.0	11,487	100.0	11,487

SOURCE: American Association of Colleges of Pharmacy (2011).

of pharmacy graduates had a BS until 2000, when about 40 percent of graduates had a BS and 60 percent had a PharmD. From 1997 to 2003, the number of graduates fluctuated, which likely shows the effects of the transition to the PharmD, as pharmacy schools transitioned at different times. Beginning in 2004, the number of graduates steadily increased through 2010. By 2010, 11,487 first professional degrees in pharmacy (PharmD) were awarded, of which 62.7 percent were to females and 37.3 percent were to males. These trends indicate that the transition to the PharmD program is likely complete and supply may continue to steadily rise with demand.

Changing demographics in the supply of pharmacists

As Table 3.6 shows, a greater proportion of females than males have studied pharmacy over the years, especially at the first professional degree level, where females made up a majority (62.7 percent) of the graduates in 2010. Some researchers have observed that as more

Table 3.6 First Professional Degrees and Graduate Degrees Conferred by Gender, 2001–2010

Year	First professional degrees (BS, PharmD)			Graduate degrees (post-BS PharmD, MS, PhD)		
	Male (%)	Female (%)	Total	Male (%)	Female (%)	Total
2001	35.5	64.5	7,000	41.9	58.1	1,815
2002	34.3	65.7	7,573	41.9	58.1	1,599
2003	35.2	64.8	7,488	42.7	57.3	1,751
2004	33.4	66.6	8,158	41.7	58.3	1,742
2005	31.9	68.1	8,268	40.0	60.0	1,723
2006	31.8	68.2	9,040	43.4	56.6	1,601
2007	32.3	67.4	9,812	37.2	62.8	1,486
2008	34.0	66.0	10,500	44.8	55.2	1,200
2009	35.6	64.4	10,988	44.4	55.6	1,753
2010	37.3	62.7	11,487	44.4	55.6	1,750

NOTE: A majority of colleges and schools (127) will offer the PharmD as a first professional degree and 11 colleges and schools will offer the PharmD as a post-BS degree in Fall 2012.
SOURCE: American Association of Colleges of Pharmacy (2011).

females enter the pharmacist workforce, there may be greater difficulty in finding full-time pharmacists because females tend to work part-time more often than males. However, the proportion of males has been increasing since 2007, so perhaps the gender divide in the pharmaceutical industry is shrinking.

ASSESSMENT OF LABOR MARKET/SHORTAGE CONDITIONS

Interviews with experts, a review of recent literature, and analysis of employment and earnings trends for pharmacists indicate that although the labor market for pharmacists has occasionally been very tight (sometimes bordering on shortages), there is not an overall current shortage. However, the literature and experts point to the complexities of determining whether there is a shortage or a tight labor market for pharmacists, because there is quite a bit of flexibility in the use of part-time labor to fill vacancies, and pharmacy hours can be altered to address staffing issues. For example, one interviewee observed the challenges to detecting shortages within such an occupation:

It can be difficult to determine if there is a shortage within an occupation. There is a need to distinguish between whether hours are fixed versus flexible for an occupation. In pharmacies, hours can be changed and you can change the mix of part-time and full-time workers. For example, a pharmacy can change its hours from 24 hours a day to 12 hours a day—there are lots of ways in which pharmacies can adjust to labor market conditions. There is less flexibility to make adjustments, on the other hand, with teachers—they normally work school days, there are fixed hours and no overtime, and pay/hours are subject to a teachers' union contract.

A second expert also pointed to the complexities of determining whether a particular area was experiencing a true shortage of pharmacists to fill available vacancies:

It is hard to tell if it is an "artificial" shortage caused by stores trying to increase hours. For example, you could have two pharmacies a mile apart (a CVS and a Rite Aid). What happens is that they try to expand hours, creating a "shortage"—that is, unfilled positions in that locality. But whether this is a shortage, depends on the definition of shortage that is applied. Chain store pharmacies often want to offer late hours so that they can serve new customers. Is there really a shortage of pharmacists if you cannot fill a prescription at 2 a.m.?

Several interviewees indicated that there have been shortages of pharmacists to fill vacancies and that tightness within the labor market continues, with some geographic areas experiencing difficulties in recruiting pharmacists to fill vacancies or staff certain hours at which a pharmacy might want to remain open. One interviewee noted that residents in rural communities might experience greater difficulties with regard to getting prescriptions filled, stating, "You might have to travel 30 miles in a rural area to fill a prescription, but only around a mile or so in an urban setting." With regard to shortages, interviewees suggested that the labor market for pharmacists was particularly tight about a decade ago (in 1999 and 2000), when educational qualifications for pharmacists were increased by one year with the shift from the bachelor's degree to the PharmD degree. This shift in educational requirements created a lag in supply in the pipeline of new pharmacists, which rippled through the labor market at a time when several other underlying factors (see the earlier discussion) were also serving to increase demand for additional pharmacists.

Interviewees and the literature suggested that there was a likelihood that the labor market for pharmacists would continue to grow and perhaps tighten in the future, but that it was unlikely that there would be shortages unless there were major changes in regulations. One interviewee observed that over the last 10 years, new pharmacy schools have opened and are now graduating their first classes, which has resulted (and will result) in an increased supply of pharmacists in the coming years to meet demand.

RESPONSES TO LABOR MARKET CONDITIONS

Although the analyses indicate there are no current shortages of pharmacists, a number of strategies have been employed in the past to respond to the tight labor market conditions for pharmacists (some or all of which could potentially be used in the future, should any shortages occur). For example, Scheckelhoff (2006) found that health-system pharmacy directors employed a variety of nontraditional staffing model practices to overcome turnover and vacancies in 2006, including the following:

- 54 percent provided options for working longer shifts and fewer days per week;

- 48 percent provided employees the option of collaborating on creating their own work schedules that would meet both individual and organizational needs;

- 45 percent provided opportunities for two part-time employees to divide the hours and responsibilities of a full-time position;

- 41 percent offered programs that supported pharmacists who were looking to transition from a community pharmacy to a health-system position;

- 18 percent provided support or incentives for retirement-age workers to remain in the workforce longer;

- 13 percent offered programs that supported pharmacists who were attempting to reenter the workforce after an extended (five years or more) absence from the profession;

- 10 percent had other employees, such as pharmacy technicians, who performed their job responsibilities from home; and

- 8 percent had pharmacists who processed patient care orders from home.

Interviews conducted for this study identified a number of strategies that employers have used in the past in responding to tight labor market conditions for pharmacists, including the following:

- **Increase wages.** According to one interviewee, raising pay has been one approach to coax new entrants into the profession, as well as a means for employers to fill vacant positions. A second analyst noted that salaries for pharmacists have increased rapidly, but fringe benefits have remained about the same.

- **Increase the use of automation.** One interviewee noted that hospitals and other employers have increasingly used automated systems to reduce pharmacists' time in filling prescriptions. This has led to productivity increases (i.e., increasing the amount of work that can be accomplished by pharmacists in the same period of time) and, at the same time, has had other benefits for customers (e.g., the software used checks for drug interactions and inappropriate levels of prescriptions). This trend toward automation has gone on for at least 15 years. These automated systems are linked to national systems that check across states for prescriptions filled. A second interviewee noted that some states do and others do not allow branch locations to prefill bottles for prescriptions. States that do not allow this require what is known as a "central fill," in which bottles for prescriptions are filled at a central location, rather than at the local pharmacy.

- **Substitute less expensive labor (pharmacy technicians/aides).** According to one interviewee, there has been increased use of pharmacy technicians or aides over the years as another way to reduce demand for pharmacists. Such technicians or aides are particularly used in chain drug stores and in larger urban areas. A second analyst observed that although states have set limits on the ratio of technicians to pharmacists, these ratios are often not binding or enforced.

- **Reduce pharmacy hours or wait times for filling prescriptions.** Some pharmacies have cut back on the hours they are open for filling prescriptions (e.g., cutting back on evening or overnight hours). Additionally, although there is no evidence (according to analysts interviewed for this study) of customers being unable to fill prescriptions, when employers are unable to fill vacancies for pharmacists, customers may encounter longer wait times in getting prescriptions filled.

- **Increase the pipeline of new workers.** A handful of new PharmD schools have been built in recent years or are currently being built, resulting in an increase in the supply of pharmacists. Also, there are some long-distance (via the Internet) training programs that enable pharmacists with a bachelor's degree to get a doctoral degree.

CONCLUSIONS AND RECOMMENDATIONS

The analyses in this chapter suggest that although there has been a tight labor market for pharmacists at times (bordering on shortages), the tightness peaked about 10 years ago, and now there appears to be a generally adequate supply of workers to meet labor market demand. However, there are some local areas (particularly rural areas) where difficulties in the recruitment of pharmacists result in patients needing to travel farther than they might want to in order to have their prescriptions filled. Some of the steps taken by employers in the past in responding to tight labor market conditions were outlined as possible actions that could be taken in the future should shortages arise.

The case study of pharmacists fits well with the economic theory presented in Chapter 1. Although subject to licensing, pharmacists are not subject to the market restrictions that special education teachers, home care workers, and physical therapists experience. Thus, although there can be (and were) market shocks that lead to shortages, the market can adjust to remedy the situation. Several factors converged to cause a temporary shortage of pharmacists about a decade ago—the increased length of schooling, the decision by many grocery stores to add pharmacies, and the decision by many pharmacy chains to increase hours are examples. The market has responded well to these developments, using many of the mechanisms predicted by the economic theory presented in Chapter 1. Although the BLS projects that the occupation will grow faster than average, the industry should be able to accommodate the growth using the mechanisms described above. The one potential roadblock that bears watching is the capacity of pharmacy schools to meet the demand for new pharmacists.

Notes

1. Some examples of Web sites with more specific listings for pharmacists or health care professionals include http://www.rxcareercenter.com, http://www.rxinsider .com, http://www.pharmacy-staffing.com, http://www.pharmacychoice.com/ careers/, healthcallings.com, and http://www.iHirePharmacy.com. An example of a company Web site with pharmacy openings is Target (http://sites.target.com/site/ en/company/page.jsp?contentId=WCMP04-030796www.findlocaljobsnow.com).
2. For example, the American Pharmacists Association has a Web site that allows for easy searching of pharmacist job openings: http://assoc.healthecareers.com/apha/ association-home/ (accessed August 28, 2010).
3. From the Ehow Web site at http://www.ehow.com/how_2068810_find-pharmacist -jobs.html#ixzz0vl8RSiFv (accessed August 28, 2010).

4

Physical Therapists

We selected physical therapists for a case study because physical therapy is a field that (along with nursing) has long been on the Department of Labor's list of occupations experiencing a national shortage.[1] In addition, the popular and academic literature has chronicled shortages in this field for more than 25 years, and the labor market for this profession is interesting for several reasons. Studies dating back to the 1950s have suggested that a significant number of physical therapists qualified to practice choose not to do so and, as in other health care occupations, there are issues of burnout and other factors that affect flow into and out of the profession (which in turn affects supply conditions). There are also interesting issues involving the number of training institutions preparing physical therapists as well as the relatively lengthy periods of education and stringent licensing requirements needed for entry. (That is to say, physical therapists need a postgraduate degree from an accredited physical therapy program and a state license, which requires passing scores on national and state examinations.)

There is also a strong push within the field for academic institutions still offering master's-degree-level training to either close their programs or shift to offering doctoral-degree training (which lengthens the duration of training from two years to three years and increases the training costs involved in becoming a licensed physical therapist).[2] As discussed below, several indicators of labor market conditions— for example, very low unemployment rates and escalating salaries— are suggestive of tight labor market conditions. In addition, there are expectations for continued employment growth in the field, with particularly strong forecasts for employment in acute hospital, rehabilitation, and orthopedic settings. There is, according to the literature, increasing specialization within the occupation, which tends to decrease the interchangeability of practitioners and increase the number of practitioners required to meet specific service needs. There are also intriguing issues regarding substitution of less skilled aides or assistants and advances in medical technology and equipment that affect demand for physical therapists—for example, as related to the appropriate blend of physical therapists to physical therapist assistants for delivery of services in various settings and for various case mixes.

BACKGROUND AND DESCRIPTION

As documented in the *Occupational Outlook Handbook*, published biennially by the BLS, physical therapists provide services that help restore function, improve mobility, relieve pain, and prevent or limit permanent physical disabilities for patients suffering from injuries or disease.[3] They restore, maintain, and promote the overall fitness and health of patients. Patients of physical therapists include accident victims and individuals with disabling conditions such as low-back pain, arthritis, heart disease, fractures, head injuries, and cerebral palsy.

Therapists typically examine patients' medical histories and then test and measure the patients' strength, range of motion, balance and coordination, posture, muscle performance, respiration, and motor function. Physical therapists develop plans describing a treatment strategy and its anticipated outcome, and then provide treatment. Physical therapists encourage patients to use their muscles to increase their flexibility and range of motion. More advanced exercises focus on improving strength, balance, coordination, and endurance. The goal is to improve how an individual functions at work and at home. Physical therapists also use electrical stimulation, hot packs or cold compresses, and ultrasound to relieve pain and reduce swelling. They may use traction or deep-tissue massage to relieve pain and improve circulation and flexibility. Therapists also teach patients to use assistive and adaptive devices, such as crutches, prostheses, and wheelchairs. They also may show patients how to do exercises at home to expedite their recovery. As treatment continues, physical therapists document the patient's progress, conduct periodic examinations, and modify treatments when necessary.

Some physical therapists treat a wide range of ailments; others specialize in areas such as pediatrics, geriatrics, orthopedics, sports medicine, neurology, and cardiopulmonary physical therapy. Physical therapists often consult and practice with a variety of other professionals, such as physicians, dentists, nurses, educators, social workers, occupational therapists, speech-language pathologists, and audiologists. In addition, physical therapist assistants and aides may help physical therapists to provide treatment; for example, a physical therapist might utilize an assistant to help patients exercise or learn to use crutches. Physical therapists practice in hospitals, clinics, and private offices that have specially equipped facilities. They also treat patients in hospital rooms, homes, or schools. Tasks performed by physical therapists can be physically demanding because therapists often have to stoop, kneel, crouch, lift, and stand for long periods. In addition, physical therapists move heavy equipment and lift patients or help them turn, stand, or walk. In 2008, most full-time physical therapists worked a 40-hour week, with some working evenings and weekends to fit their patients' schedules, and about 27 percent worked part-time (BLS 2010c).

The *Occupational Outlook Handbook* distinguishes the duties of physical therapist assistants versus physical therapist aides as follows. Under the direction and supervision of physical therapists, physical therapist assistants provide part of a patient's treatment, which might involve exercises, massages, electrical stimulation, paraffin baths, hot and cold packs, traction, and ultrasound. Physical therapist assistants record the patient's responses to treatment and report the outcome of each treatment to the physical therapist. Physical therapist aides help make therapy sessions productive, under the direct supervision of a physical therapist or physical therapist assistant. They usually are responsible for keeping the treatment area clean and organized and for preparing for each patient's therapy. When patients need assistance moving to or from a treatment area, aides push them in a wheelchair or provide them with a shoulder to lean on. Because they are not licensed, aides do not perform the clinical tasks of a physical therapist assistant in states where licensure is required. The duties of aides may also include some clerical tasks, such as ordering supplies, answering the phone, and filling out insurance forms and other paperwork. The extent to which an aide or an assistant performs clerical tasks typically depends on the size and location of the facility.

In the United States, physical therapists formed their first professional association in 1921, called the American Women's Physical Therapeutic Association. By the end of the 1930s, the Association changed its name to the American Physiotherapy Association.[4] With the advent of World War II and its hundreds of thousands of wounded soldiers, as well as a nationwide polio epidemic during the 1940s and 1950s, the demand for physical therapists intensified. Treatment through the 1940s primarily consisted of exercise, massage, and traction; in the early 1950s came increasing use of manipulative procedures to the spine and extremity joints. Also beginning in the 1950s, physical therapists moved beyond hospital-based practice to outpatient orthopedic clinics, skilled nursing facilities (SNFs), rehabilitation centers, and other facilities. Over the past half-century, there has been increasing specialization in the field of physical therapy, as well as the emergence of physical therapist assistants and aides. The American Physical Therapy Association (APTA) established the specialist certification program in 1978 in recognition of the increasing specialization within the field of physical therapy. According to the APTA Web site, APTA has developed specialist certification programs in the following specialty areas: cardiopulmonary, clinical electrophysiology, geriatrics, neurology, orthopedics, pediatrics, and sports physical therapy.[5]

TRAINING AND RECRUITMENT OF WORKERS

This section discusses the educational requirements and qualifications for entry into the physical therapist occupation, the factors affecting those requirements, and the employment characteristics of physical therapists. This examination of the means by which individuals enter the occupation lays the groundwork for the later analysis of labor market conditions.

Educational Qualifications and Entry Requirements

The minimum educational requirement is a postbaccalaureate degree from an accredited educational program. After graduation, candidates must also pass a state-administered national exam. Other requirements for physical therapy practice vary from state to state according to physical therapy practice acts or state regulations governing physical therapy. According to APTA, as of January 2011 there were 212 accredited physical therapist education programs in the United States. Of the accredited programs, nine offered master's degrees (MS/MPT) and 203 offered doctoral degrees (DPT).[6] Only master's and doctoral degree programs are accredited, in accordance with the Commission on Accreditation in Physical Therapy Education. APTA has set a goal that, by 2020, the doctoral degree will be the only acceptable degree for entry.[7]

Master's degree programs typically last two years, while doctoral degree programs last three. Most doctoral and master's degree programs require students to enter with an undergraduate degree, although some will admit students after three years of undergraduate work and a few admit students at the freshman level.[8] Physical therapist education programs start with basic science courses such as biology, chemistry, and physics and then introduce specialized courses, including biomechanics, neuroanatomy, human growth and development, manifestations of disease, examination techniques, and therapeutic procedures. Besides receiving classroom and laboratory instruction, students receive supervised clinical experience (BLS 2010c).

Methods Employers Use to Recruit Workers and Workers Use to Obtain Employment

Employers, such as acute care facilities, SNFs, and agency providers, recruit new physical therapists through interactions with universities providing postgraduate training programs. These employers may also recruit new entries to the field at professional conferences or by placing advertisements in professional publications and on Web sites. Word of mouth also plays a role in the recruitment of newly trained physical therapists, as well as in recruiting physical therapists already working within the field but contemplating a change. Like many other health care providers, physical therapist employers utilize their own Web sites to advertise job openings, as well as advertising job openings on various health care and general employment Web sites. For example, there are quite a few Web sites that specialize in helping physical therapists to find job openings, including the following:[9]

- TherapyJobBoard.com hosts job postings from therapy employers and staffing agencies around the country. The services are free for job seekers.
- Therapyjobs.com offers a list of physical therapy jobs alphabetically by state. This site gives a description of each job listed. Job seekers can also post their resumes for employers to look at.

- JobsinTherapy.com allows the user to be more specific in his or her job search—allowing, for example, the user to search for physical therapy jobs by state and setting.

- RehabWorld.com is another Web site that allows the user to look for physical therapy jobs by state.

These Web sites typically make it very easy for candidates to apply for job vacancies and to contact job recruiters.

Additionally, physical therapy associations have set up electronic bulletin boards to list vacancies available for physical therapy positions. For example, APTA has an interactive site devoted to connecting physical therapists with employers that have job vacancies.[10] The APTA Web site provides the physical therapist with the capability to search for available job openings based on practice setting (e.g., academic institution, acute care hospital, or health and wellness facility); practice area (e.g., acute care hospital/clinical practice, aquatic physical therapy, and cardiovascular/pulmonary); job type (e.g., full time, part time, internship, and contract); state; and job source (agency placement or company placement). The APTA Web site also provides job applicants with help developing resumes and letters, a listing of job search resources, the ability to receive "job alerts," and the capability to post a resume that can be viewed by prospective employers. A portion of the APTA Web site is devoted to helping employers find physical therapists to fill job openings, including the ability for employers to post job openings, view resumes, and post advertisements.

WORKER CHARACTERISTICS

The basic demographic characteristics of physical therapists are shown in Table 4.1. As shown in the table, among the defining characteristics of physical therapists (i.e., those who are members of APTA) are the following (APTA 2011a):

- About two-thirds are women (68.3 percent).
- A very high proportion are white (92.7 percent), with relatively few minorities represented.

- More than half (52.2 percent) are between the ages of 25 and 44, although slightly more than one-third are 50 or older (34.3 percent).

- Although schools and the APTA are pushing to make doctoral training (i.e., the DPT) the norm by 2020, most APTA members had either a baccalaureate (47.1 percent) or a master's (30.2 percent) degree at the time of their entry into the physical therapy field (17.3 percent had a DPT).

- Some 57.9 percent of physical therapists are full-time salaried employees, and an additional 4.7 percent are part-time salaried employees.

- At the time of the survey (2010), 0.8 percent of APTA members indicated they were not employed (with half of these individuals indicating that they were seeking work).

- Most APTA members work in one of three types of facilities: private outpatient office or group practices (33.6 percent), health-system or hospital-based outpatient facilities or clinics (20.9 percent), or acute care hospitals (11.4 percent).

APTA has also conducted surveys to examine turnover rates among physical therapists in three practice settings: acute care hospitals, SNFs, and outpatient physical therapy offices. With regard to acute care hospitals, APTA sent survey instruments to 2,000 hospitals that house a department of physical therapy and received 703 responses. Turnover rates were computed separately for full- and part-time physical therapists (within acute care hospitals), as well as for full- and part-time physical therapist assistants. Turnover was computed by dividing the number of employees within a specific category who left in the most recent 12-month period by the number of employees within that category, and doing this for each respective category at the facility. The turnover rate for full-time physical therapists was 11.9 percent, compared to a rate of 9.0 percent for part-time physical therapists, 10.4 percent for full-time physical therapist assistants, and 9.6 percent for part-time physical therapist assistants. In 2007, the APTA survey found substantial variability across acute care hospitals, with some facilities reporting very high turnover rates among physical therapists—12 facilities reported turnover rates of 100 percent, one a rate of 150 percent, and another a

Table 4.1 Overview of Characteristics of Physical Therapists, 2010

Demographic characteristic	% of APTA members
Gender	
Female	68.3
Male	31.7
Race/ethnicity	
White	92.7
Asian	4.7
African American/black	1.4
Other	1.2
Ethnic origin	
Hispanic or Latino	2.1
Not Hispanic or Latino	97.9
Age	
20–24	0.8
25–29	13.4
30–34	13.2
35–39	12.8
40–44	12.8
45–49	12.6
50–59	25.5
60+	8.8
Entry-level education	
DPT	17.3
Master's	30.2
Baccalaureate	47.1
Postbaccalaureate certificate	3.3
Other	2.1
Employment status	
Full-time salaried	57.9
Part-time salaried	4.7
Full-time hourly	12.9
Part-time hourly	7.5
Full-time self-employed	12.3
Part-time self-employed	2.8
Retired	1.0
Unemployed—seeking work	0.4
Unemployed—not seeking work[a]	0.4

Table 4.1 (continued)

Demographic characteristic	% of APTA members
Type of facility	
Private outpatient office or group practice	33.6
Health system–based or hospital-based outpatient facility/clinic	20.9
Acute care hospital	11.4
Patient's home/home care	6.8
Skilled nursing facility (SNF)/long-term care	5.1
Academic institution (postsecondary)	9.6
School system (preschool, primary, secondary)	3.6
Inpatient rehab facility (IRF)	3.0
Health and wellness facility	0.5
Industry	0.5
Research center	0.2
Other	4.7

NOTE: Demographics are for physical therapists that are members of APTA (APTA 2011a). Numbers for demographic characteristics may not sum to 100.0 because of rounding.

[a] The APTA table on the Web site calls the category "Unemployed—not seeking work." However, this is technically a misnomer, since a person must be actively seeking work to count as officially unemployed. Regardless, this line counts people who have no job and are not seeking work.

rate of 200 percent. APTA found high turnover rates particularly among recent entrants to the field of physical therapy: "There seemed to be a sharp dichotomy in the decision to leave based on years of experience. Individuals with four years or less of experience were more likely to leave a position than those with longer tenure" (APTA 2008).

By 2010, however, turnover rates for physical therapists in acute care hospitals had declined by about 3 percentage points. This is most likely because recessionary economic conditions encouraged health care workers to remain in their current positions.

The APTA also surveyed SNFs and based its findings on 481 survey responses from these facilities. Using the same definition for turnover as in its survey of acute care hospitals, the APTA found a much higher turnover rate for physical therapists in SNFs as compared to acute care hospitals. The most recent turnover rate available was 27.6

percent for full-time physical therapists in SNFs in 2009—much higher than the 11.9 percent reported for full-time physical therapists in acute care hospitals. Twenty-seven percent is, however, substantially lower than the 85.2 percent turnover rate that was reported for full-time physical therapists in SNFs the last time this survey was conducted in 2006. The turnover rate among full-time physical therapist assistants in SNFs was 22.9 percent, which again had declined substantially from the 82.4 percent reported in the previous survey of full-time physical therapist assistants in SNFs. This survey found that although "the distribution of individuals who left a position (in an SNF) was skewed in the direction of more junior personnel, there were a number of more senior individuals who left as well" (APTA 2011b). The APTA reported that length of experience and turnover rate did not seem to have a relationship in SNFs. This is similar to the findings for acute care settings, where turnover rates were similar for junior and more senior therapists in 2009. (This trend has notably changed since prior studies, which found that turnover rates were typically much higher among junior staff in acute care settings.) Additionally, by 2009, a substantially lower number of individuals were reported to have left their positions than in the 2006 survey results.

EMPLOYMENT AND EARNINGS TRENDS

Employment Trends

Employment levels and change

Data from the BLS indicate a steady increase in the number of workers employed as physical therapists in recent years, as well as anticipated increases in employment through 2016. As shown in Table 4.2, the number of wage and salary jobs as physical therapists in the United States increased from 156,100 in 2006 to 180,280 positions in 2010—an increase of more than 24,000 jobs. Overall, the total number of wage and salary positions increased by 15.5 percent over the time period. The increase in employment was at a somewhat faster pace for physical therapists as compared to all health care practitioners and tech-

Table 4.2 Number of and Percentage Change in Physical Therapists, Comparison Occupations, and All Workers, 2006–2010

Occupation	2006	2007	2008	2009	2010	% change
Physical therapists	156,100	161,850	167,300	174,490	180,280	15.5
Occupational therapists	88,570	91,920	94,800	97,840	100,300	13.2
Chiropractors	25,470	27,190	27,050	26,310	26,250	3.1
Registered nurses	2,417,150	2,468,340	2,542,760	2,583,770	2,655,020	9.8
All health care practitioners and technical occupations	6,713,780	6,877,680	7,076,800	7,200,950	7,346,580	9.4
Physical therapist assistants	59,350	59,120	61,820	63,750	65,960	11.1
Physical therapist aides	45,520	43,350	44,410	44,160	45,900	0.8
Occupational therapist assistants	23,700	25,130	25,610	26,680	27,720	17.0
Occupational therapist aides	7,780	7,640	7,410	8,040	7,180	−7.7
All health care support occupations	3,483,270	3,625,240	3,779,280	3,886,690	3,962,930	13.8
All workers from all occupations	132,604,980	134,354,250	135,185,230	130,647,610	127,097,160	−4.2

SOURCE: 2006–2009 data: BLS (2011a); 2010 data: BLS (2011b).

nical occupations (13.8 percent). Notably, by comparison, employment for all workers from all occupations actually declined in number and in percentage terms (by 4.2 percent) during the same time period.

The pace of increase in employment was more rapid for physical therapists over the five-year period (15.5 percent) as compared to physical therapist assistants (11.1 percent) and physical therapist aides (0.8 percent). The percentage increase for physical therapists was also greater than that experienced by registered nurses (9.8 percent) and occupational therapists (13.2 percent), but lower than that for occupational therapist assistants (17.0 percent). Overall, the rapid increase in employment for physical therapists over the past five years suggests strong and sustained demand for physical therapists and the possibility of a tight labor market.

Unemployment rates

As illustrated in Table 4.3, the unemployment rate for physical therapists—as for most health care practitioners and technical occupations—is well below the average for all U.S. workers. For example, in 2010, the unemployment rate for physical therapists was 2.0 percent, as compared to 8.9 percent for all workers from all occupations. Over the five years shown in the table (2006–2010), the unemployment rate for physical therapists was consistently very low (e.g., averaging 1.3 percent and not exceeding 2.0 percent) and relatively stable. In fact, in 2010, the unemployment rate for physical therapists was nearly 7 percentage points lower than that for all workers. The unemployment rate for physical therapists was also consistently lower than that of registered nurses, an occupation that has historically been judged as suffering from a persistently tight labor market. Other things being equal, most analysts would consider the relatively low unemployment rate for physical therapists to be potentially indicative of tightness or shortages within that occupation.

In comparison to trends for physical therapists, the unemployment rates for physical therapist assistants and aides have been much more volatile over the five-year period. In 2006 and 2007, the field had a very low unemployment rate (less than 1 percent), especially when compared to the rate for all workers and even the rate for all health care support occupations. In 2008, the unemployment rate for physical

Table 4.3 Average Annual Unemployment Rate (%) for Physical Therapists, Comparison Occupations, and All Workers, 2006–2010

Occupation	2006	2007	2008	2009	2010
Physical therapists	1.0	0.5	0.9	1.9	2.0
Occupational therapists	0.2	1.6	1.4	1.8	1.0
Registered nurses	1.1	1.0	1.2	2.1	2.1
All health care practitioners and technical occupations	1.4	1.3	1.5	2.3	2.5
Nursing, psychiatric, and home health aides	5.6	5.2	5.2	7.4	9.2
Physical therapist assistants and aides	0.6	0.4	7.1	6.3	3.5
All health care support occupations	4.6	4.5	4.5	6.8	7.6
All workers from all occupations	4.2	4.2	5.3	8.6	8.9

SOURCE: Unpublished BLS Survey from the Current Population Survey (2006–2010), Table 3: Annual average employed and experienced unemployed persons by detailed occupation and class of worker.

therapist assistants and aides suddenly jumped from 0.4 percent to 7.1 percent, most likely because of the severe recession. However, by 2010, the unemployment rate for physical therapist assistants and aides had fallen back to 3.5 percent, about half the rate recorded for 2008.

Vacancy rates

APTA has examined vacancy rates among physical therapists in three practice settings: acute care hospitals, SNFs, and outpatient physical therapy offices. Using survey results, APTA calculated vacancy rates by "dividing the total number of vacant FTE [full-time equivalent] positions by the total number of vacant FTE positions plus the total number of filled FTE positions and multiplying by 100" (APTA 2010a). The 2010 APTA survey research found that the vacancy rate for physical therapists in acute care hospitals was 10.0 percent. The Physical Therapy Workforce Project (Long-Term Care) 2011 (APTA 2010b) found that the vacancy rate for physical therapists in long-term care settings was 12.1 percent and that the vacancy rate for physical therapists in outpatient settings was 11.2 percent. APTA cites two additional but somewhat older studies of vacancy rates for physical therapists for comparison purposes: 1) the vacancy rate for hospital-based physical therapists in Maryland was 17.1 percent (as reported by the Maryland Hospital Association); and 2) the vacancy index for physical therapists (across all settings) in North Carolina computed by analyzing job advertisements was 14.8 percent (Fraher et al. 2007; Maryland Hospital Association 2007). According to one interviewee for this study, high vacancy rates and "much of the shortage (for physical therapists) was a result of the Balanced Budget Act (BBA) of 1997: (1) lower reimbursement rates led to changes in staffing—physical therapists had benefits cut and hours reduced; (2) [the] profession became less attractive to potential physical therapists; and (3) [the] 'pipeline' decreased and supply of physical therapists diminished."

Projections for future employment growth within the occupation

As also shown in Table 4.4, the BLS forecasts that the number of workers employed as physical therapists will increase by 34.1 percent from 2010 to 2018. By 2018, there will be a total of 241,700 physical therapists employed (an increase of 61,420 new therapists over the nine-year period). By comparison, overall employment for all occupations in the United States is expected to expand by 30.8 percent, and that of all health care practitioners and technical occupations by 23.7 percent. The anticipated rate of increase for physical therapists is also above that for occupational therapists (30.9 percent) and registered nurses (20.5 percent). The projected increase for physical therapist assistants (28.9 percent) and physical therapist aides (36.8 percent) is similar to that for physical therapists, indicating that there will likely be continued strong demand well into the future not only for physical therapists, but also for the two occupational categories that work closely with and support physical therapists.

BLS's general assessment is that employment for physical therapists is expected to grow faster than the average for all occupations: "Job opportunities will be good for licensed physical therapists in all settings. Job opportunities should be particularly good in acute hospital, skilled nursing, and orthopedic settings, where the elderly are most

**Table 4.4 Employment for Physical Therapists, Comparison Occupations,
and All Workers, 2010 and 2018 (projected)**

Occupation	2010	Projected 2018	% change
Physical therapists	180,280	241,700	34.1
Occupational therapists	100,300	131,300	30.9
Registered nurses	2,655,020	3,200,200	20.5
All health care practitioners and technical occupations	7,346,580	9,090,800	23.7
Physical therapist assistants	65,960	85,000	28.9
Physical therapist aides	45,900	62,800	36.8
Occupational therapist assistants	27,720	34,600	24.8
Occupational therapist aides	7,180	10,200	42.1
All health care support occupations	3,962,930	5,129,500	29.4
All workers from all occupations	127,097,160	166,205,600	30.8

SOURCE: BLS (2010c).

often treated. Job prospects should be especially favorable in rural areas as many physical therapists tend to cluster in highly populated urban and suburban areas" (BLS 2010c).

Earnings Trends

The rate at which wages rise within an occupation is often viewed as the clearest indication of whether a shortage of workers exists (at least over the short term, and providing there are not constraints on wages). Table 4.5 shows median hourly earnings for physical therapists from 2006 to 2010. Earnings for physical therapists are more than twice those for all workers (e.g., in 2010, the median hourly earnings for physical therapists were $36.69, versus $16.27 for all workers). The increase in median hourly earnings for physical therapists between 2006 and 2010 (15.3 percent) was well above that for all workers (11.4 percent). This earnings increase for physical therapists over the five-year period was at about the same level as that of all health care practitioners and technical occupations (12.5 percent), as well as that of

Table 4.5 Median Hourly Earnings ($) for Physical Therapists, Comparison Occupations, and All Workers, 2006–2010

	2006	2007	2008	2009	2010	% change
Physical therapists	31.83	33.54	35.00	35.81	36.69	15.3
Occupational therapists	29.07	30.67	32.10	33.48	34.77	19.6
Registered nurses	27.54	28.85	30.03	30.65	31.10	12.9
All health care practitioners and technical occupations	24.99	26.17	27.20	27.74	28.12	12.5
Physical therapist assistants	19.88	21.22	22.18	23.22	23.89	20.2
Physical therapist aides	10.61	11.05	11.42	11.49	11.39	7.4
Occupational therapist assistants	20.22	21.66	23.19	24.16	24.66	22.0
Occupational therapist aides	12.03	12.54	12.96	12.37	13.19	9.6
All health care support occupations	11.00	11.45	11.80	14.39	14.56	32.4
All workers from all occupations	14.61	15.10	15.57	15.95	16.27	11.4

SOURCE: BLS (2010d, 2011a).

occupational therapists (19.6 percent) and registered nurses (12.9 percent). Also shown in the table are increases in hourly earnings for occupational therapist assistants (22.0 percent), physical therapist assistants (20.2 percent), and physical therapist aides (7.4 percent). Hourly wages for physical therapist assistants in 2010 were about two-thirds of wages of physical therapists ($23.89 versus $36.69), and those for physical therapist aides were about one-third those of physical therapists ($11.39 versus $36.69). Above-average increases in hourly earnings, similar to trends in employment and unemployment, suggest the possibility of a tight labor market for physical therapists—although, as discussed later, because of possible distortions in reimbursement rates (related to government reimbursements for physical therapist–provided services), the earnings increases may not fully measure the extent of tightness or shortage in the labor market for physical therapists.

LABOR MARKET FACTORS CONTRIBUTING TO A LABOR SHORTAGE

Demand-Side Factors

Changes to reimbursement for physical therapy services

In its assessment, the BLS noted that "changes to restrictions on reimbursement for physical therapy services by third-party payers will increase patient access to services and, thus, increase demand" (BLS 2010c). Recent history provides much evidence that third-party insurance coverage and reimbursement policies have a substantial impact on demand for and utilization of physical therapy services. The literature and interviews conducted as part of this study point to the increasingly important role of legislation and federal regulation (particularly of reimbursement rates and coverage limitations) in determining labor market conditions for physical therapy services. Several interviewees highlighted the importance of Medicare, and to a lesser extent Medicaid (because both programs are such important sources of payment for physical therapy service), in establishing the basic framework for reimbursement of physical therapy services. The terms of what is and is not reimbursable under Medicare and the payment rates are also often adopted by other major health care insurers,[11] which makes government actions all the more important and determinant.[12] Several interviewees pointed to the particularly important role of the BBA in determining policies with regard to Medicare reimbursement and substantially affecting labor market conditions for physical therapists. For example, according to one interviewee,

> The Medicare system has a huge impact on supply and demand conditions for physical therapists. The Balanced Budget Act (BBA) of 1997 introduced dramatic changes for payment for physical therapy (and other medical services) by home health care agencies and skilled nursing facilities (SNFs). Prior to BBA, payments were based on actual costs, which incentivized facilities to hire physical therapists and pay them a lot. Prior to BBA, health care facilities were paid a percentage of costs (usually 80 percent). With BBA, cost-based payment changed to a fixed rate per case, with payment based on resource utilization groups (RUGs). Basically, facilities were paid a flat rate set at the time of admission—usually about $350 per day, which covered the full cost of medicine, therapy, bed, etc., so facilities immediately cut back on physical therapists, occupational therapists, etc. Overall, the BBA created strong incentives to cut back on use of physical therapists, resulting in a drastic reduction in hours worked by physical therapists. Large numbers of physical therapists left the field in 1997—with many retiring—and so, there was a tremendous drop in physical therapists in the field.[13]

Once again, in 2002, a change in Medicare policy had a substantial effect on the demand for physical therapists (though in the opposite direction of the BBA with respect to physical therapists). Medicare introduced the "three-hour rule" for physical therapy services provided in acute rehabilitation hospitals. This rule meant that to be reimbursed for rehabilitation services, acute care facilities had to provide patients with three hours of aggressive therapy five of seven days in a week. According to one interviewee (an executive at a rehabilitation hospital):

> This new rule resulted in a surge in demand for physical therapists within acute rehabilitation hospitals . . . As a result, from about 2002 to 2008, acute rehabilitation hospitals faced shortages of physical therapists, and many of these facilities had to work with contract agencies to obtain needed physical therapists (and agen-

cies did well in those days). Medicare also introduced minimum standards of care whereby rehabilitation services need to be provided by certified physical therapists. While there are a lot of drivers when it comes to supply and demand conditions for physical therapists, the really big driver is government policies, especially, individual state practice acts and Medicare reimbursement levels and what is allowed.

One emerging trend that could result in additional demand for physical therapy services is that APTA (along with other groups representing physical therapists) is working hard with Medicare to gain direct payment for physical therapy services, without the need for referral first from a doctor.[14]

Aging of the population

One of the most prominent factors cited in the literature (and in interviews conducted for this study) with respect to driving future demand for physical therapy services is the rapid aging of the U.S. population. For example, two of the main factors cited by the BLS (2010c) for strong future growth in the demand for physical therapists are related to the aging of the U.S. population:

1) "The increasing elderly population will drive growth in the demand for physical therapy services. The elderly population is particularly vulnerable to chronic and debilitating conditions that require therapeutic services."

2) "The baby-boom generation is entering the prime age for heart attacks and strokes, increasing the demand for cardiac and physical rehabilitation."

The population in the United States that is 65 years or older has grown substantially in recent years and is expected to continue to grow rapidly over the next quarter of a century. In 2009, the most recent date for which data are available, there were an estimated 39.6 million elderly (people aged 65 or older). This is a 12.5 percent increase in the number of people in that age group since 1999, when there were 35.3 million. In 2009, people over 65 years of age made up 12.9 percent of the U.S. population, equivalent to one in every eight Americans; by 2030, this age bracket is expected to grow to 19 percent of the total population (DHHS 2010). In addition, 5.7 million Americans were over the age of 85 in 2008, and this number is projected to grow to 6.6 million by 2020.

A majority of Americans aged 65 or older have at least one chronic health condition and, depending upon the condition, may require physical therapy services over a prolonged period. In 2009, nearly 37 percent of older people reported having some type of disability. This number was very similar in 2005, and 16 percent reported that they needed assistance as a result. In addition, chronic conditions and disabilities increase with age—56 percent of people over 80 years of age reported a severe disability in 2005 (DHHS 2010). The recent and expected growth in the proportion of older Americans is significant because older people tend to need and spend more on health care and, in particular, are much more likely to require physical therapy services than younger individuals. Several of the interviewees for this study pointed to the likelihood that the aging of the baby boomers would have a big impact in coming years on utilization of physical therapy services. For example, one interviewee representing a physical therapy association observed the following: "We think shortages will continue due to aging of population (which is likely to increase demand for physical therapy services); also there is likely to be increased demand for physical therapy services with longer lifespans and a trend toward healthier lifestyles and wellness."

Medical and technological developments

According to the BLS, "medical and technological developments will permit a greater percentage of trauma victims and newborns with birth defects to survive, creating additional demand for rehabilitative care. In addition, growth may result from advances in medical technology and the use of evidence-based practices, which could permit the treatment of an increasing number of disabling conditions that were untreatable in the past" (BLS 2010c). In addition, although not a new factor, IDEA guarantees that students have access to services from physical therapists and other therapeutic and rehabilitative services. The argument here is that, as a result of new medical advances, infants, youth, and adults who might otherwise have succumbed to a disease will live longer but in some cases still require ongoing medical treatment and physical therapy.

There is, interestingly, a flip side to this argument—it is possible that robotics and other advances in medical technology in the future could reduce the need for prolonged physical therapy services or even that new devices could in some way substitute for physical therapy services. The potential for a "substitution" effect to reduce demand for physical therapist services was noted as a possibility by one interviewee: "There have been some technology substitutions in recent years, such as robotic devices (e.g., which help with walking training). Employers are particularly looking to implement strategies to enhance efficiency of physical therapists, such as implementing strategies that enable physical therapists to take care of more than one patient at a time."

Supply-Side Factors

Adequacy of the pipeline of new physical therapists and meeting escalating educational requirements

Over the past 20 years, as discussed earlier, educational requirements for entry into the field of physical therapy have escalated. Although it is possible to practice as a physical therapist without a doctoral degree, there are very few academic institutions that continue to offer a master's degree in physical therapy, because nearly all have moved to doctoral-degree-level training programs. Furthermore, reflecting recent trends within academic institutions, APTA has set a goal that the majority of practicing physical therapists will possess a doctoral degree by 2020. Escalating educational requirements—and the added costs of completing training, especially if there is not a sufficient pay differential for those attaining higher degrees within a field—can result in fewer people entering programs and completing educational requirements, as well as delaying therapists' entry into the field. Several interviewees noted how requirements have changed fairly dramatically in recent years and the possible effects of this over time on the stream of physical therapists entering the field. One interviewee described the factors at work here:

> A problem on the supply side is that there are efforts to inflate academic credentials for entry into the physical therapy field. It used to require a bachelor's degree (when I started) and then a master's degree; there are efforts now to require a doctor's degree.

This inflation in degree requirements (BA to master's to doctorate) means delaying entry of an existing cohort of students into the field. Physical therapists and professional societies are pushing advanced degrees (i.e., doctorate programs) as part of the licensing requirements. They also want physical therapists to be independent practitioners—that is, get patients without referrals from doctors, be able to bill insurers on their own, and generally get more control over their work.

With regard to expanding the pipeline of new physical therapists, this interviewee noted that there is also a logistical challenge to increasing the capacity of physical therapy programs—educational institutions need to have the available faculty and also need hands-on training, which can be difficult to arrange.

The location of education programs and the types of specialty training provided can also be factors in terms of possible shortages of physical therapists in certain localities or regions of the country or in certain specialty areas within physical therapy. For example, one interviewee noted that in rural areas it can be much more challenging to recruit physical therapists than in other areas:

Within states, rural areas tend to have a harder time recruiting physical therapists. The largest cities, such as Boston, New York, and Philadelphia, have no shortages because these cities are desirable to practitioners and there are lots of PT schools (e.g., Philadelphia has about seven schools that provide a steady pipeline of new physical therapists). Small community hospitals (in rural areas) have a tough time competing with hospitals in urban areas, so they sometimes offer huge signing bonuses for physical therapists. Even with such incentives, rural areas often have trouble attracting sufficient numbers of physical therapists. These rural areas also can have high concentrations of elderly individuals in need of physical therapy.

The changing pool of workers entering the field, part-time employment, and turnover within the field

The supply of workers within the field can be affected by rates of turnover of existing workers within the field and the extent to which physical therapists work full- or part-time hours. One expert noted that while the field of physical therapy had been dominated by women for many years, women are increasingly entering other fields, posing potential implications for future recruitment into physical therapy programs: "The supply-side can be a problem. There are some problems attracting students into the PT field. It used to be that teachers, nurses, and physical therapy were fields that women would go into. Now there are a lot of other fields women are entering."

The field of physical therapy is one that is conducive to part-time (as well as full-time) work. Similar to nursing, at any point in time, there may be a considerable number of individuals with credentials to provide physical therapy services who are not actively working in the field or who choose to work part time or with a limited number of patients. Also, turnover rates of physical therapists, particularly within certain settings, can result in a large number of job vacancies within the field. For example, the previously discussed APTA surveys found particularly high turnover for physical therapists in SNFs (see the section "Worker Characteristics," starting on p. 114).

ASSESSMENT OF LABOR MARKET/SHORTAGE CONDITIONS

The consensus, both within the literature and among experts interviewed for this study, is that although there have been times in the past where there have been very tight labor markets (bordering on shortages), there is not a nationwide shortage of physical therapists at the current time. However, there are some regions and localities within the country where employers of physical therapists have a hard time filling vacancies, particularly for some subspecialties within the field.

Several of the interviewees for this study noted past tight labor markets for physical therapists, at times bordering on shortage conditions. For example, one expert indicated the labor market had from time to time been hit by very tight conditions:

> Throughout my career (spanning 30+ years), shortages of physical therapists have been a problem. Shortages can drive the price (salaries) of physical therapists up. Over the last 20 years, there have been phases during which "rehab" hospitals and other employers have had to import physical therapists from the Philippines, Ireland, and other countries.

As noted, several interviewees pointed to shortages of physical therapists within certain geographic areas, especially rural areas and those areas that are far from training institutions:

> There is no overall shortage of physical therapists—the shortage is regional; rural areas are the main places where shortages exist. The physical therapy profession is urban and school centric; for example, Boston has four physical therapy programs (which graduate 300–400 physical therapists per year), so there is no shortage of physical therapists in Boston. As a result of supply and demand conditions, salaries for physical therapists are not as high in Boston. With regard to specific types of facilities, there is much more of a shortage of physical therapists at skilled nursing facilities.

A second analyst pointed to the difficulties that certain types of facilities, especially skilled nursing homes and long-term care (LTC) facilities, can encounter in filling job vacancies and, once filled, holding on to workers:

> Shortages today are worse in some settings than others, especially SNFs and long-term care facilities. Students often graduate from schools and immediately go into acute care facilities because they feel that they will gain the most experience and be most employable in the future. However, some have a relatively short tenure in the acute care hospitals and move to other settings. SNFs and LTC facilities seem to face the most difficulty in recruiting and keeping physical therapists. These institutions have increased salaries and benefits in an effort to attract and keep physical therapists; however, raising salaries has not been that effective in attracting physical therapists to these facilities. Relative to other settings (such as private practice), SNFs and LTC facilities face shortages mainly because working conditions are more difficult (and can be depressing).

Another analyst noted that pediatric physical therapists are difficult to find sometimes, as well as those with "certain exotic skill sets." This analyst also echoed the sentiment that nursing homes often have more difficulties with respect to recruiting and keeping physical therapists —and as a result, are more likely to rely upon contract agencies for staffing. Nursing homes also may not have the need or infrastructure to support a full-time physical therapist, and therefore may be looking to recruit one or two part-time therapists. One advantage of using contract agencies is that employers do not have to worry about a physical therapist leaving or going on vacation (thereby leaving the employer without coverage of that service).

Finally, one analyst noted that for the field of physical therapy, as for many other occupations, general economic conditions can have a substantial effect on labor market conditions and especially turnover: "With the onset of the recession in 2008, physical therapists have generally been staying put at their current jobs."

Notes

1. The U.S. Department of Labor has determined that there are not sufficient U.S. workers who are able, willing, qualified, and available as physical therapists and that the wages and working conditions of U.S. workers similarly employed will not be adversely affected by the employment of aliens.
2. Accredited physical therapy programs in the United States are either offering a doctor of physical therapy degree or planning to offer one after the American Physical Therapy Association (APTA) made a formal announcement about raising the educational standards for practitioners, who are now expected to be doctors of physical therapy by 2020 (University of Dayton, "Addressing Shortage of Physical Therapists," available at http://www.udayton.edu/news/articles/2006/01/Addressing_Shortage_of_Physical_Therapists.php, accessed January 6, 2006).
3. For additional details about the physical therapist occupation, as well as physical therapy assistants and aides, see BLS (2010a). The background information in this section relating to the nature of the work, training, and other qualifications, and the outlook for future labor market conditions for this field, are based in part on the discussion in this handbook.
4. By the late 1940s, the Association had changed its name to its current one—the American Physical Therapy Association, or APTA. By the 1960s, APTA's membership had reached 15,000, and as of 2008, membership had reached more than 75,000 individuals. A portion of the background presented in this section is from the APTA Web site (www.apta.org, accessed August 22, 2010).
5. The established minimum eligibility requirements to sit for the specialist certification examinations comprise two items: 1) current licensure to practice physical therapy in the United States, the District of Columbia, Puerto Rico, or the Virgin Islands; and 2) evidence of a minimum of 2,000 hours of clinical practice in the specialty area, 25 percent of which must have occurred within the last three years. As of 2009, there were 9,409 physical therapists who had been certified as clinical specialists, with over half (58 percent) in the specialty area of orthopedics (see http://www.abpts.org/Certification/About/MinimumRequirements/, accessed August 22, 2010).

6. From the APTA Web site (http://www.apta.org/PTEducation/Overview/, accessed August 14, 2011).
7. APTA's "Vision Sentence for Physical Therapy 2020" reads as follows: "By 2020, physical therapy will be provided by physical therapists who are doctors of physical therapy, recognized by consumers and other health care professionals as the practitioners of choice to whom consumers have direct access for the diagnosis of, interventions for, and prevention of impairments, functional limitations, and disabilities related to movement, function, and health" (http://www.apta.org/Vision2020/, accessed March 15, 2011).
8. An APTA survey of schools found that prerequisite courses for entry into postgraduate physical therapy programs vary, with more than half of the programs requiring courses such as anatomy and physiology, chemistry, physics, statistics, psychology, and general biology.
9. The Web sites identified are taken from the following site: http://physicaltherapy.about.com/od/joblistings/a/PTjobs.htm (accessed April 14, 2012).
10. The URL is http://www.apta.org/applications/CareerCenter.aspx (accessed on August 14, 2011).
11. As noted by one interviewee, "Government policy (especially Medicare policy) drives private insurance policies—private insurers tag along and implement Medicare policies."
12. A large share of physical therapy services are paid for by the government. One expert estimated that about half of physical therapy services are paid by Medicare and another 20 percent by Medicaid.
13. According to a second interviewee, "The lower reimbursement rate as a result of BBA led to an immediate response on the part of employers—since revenues were lower, employers (health care facilities) cut back expenses. Reducing staffing expenses was one way to cut back such expenses—employers cut back hours and fringe benefits of physical therapists. There was an immediate surplus of physical therapists as a result. The numbers of physical therapists applying to, enrolling [in], and graduating from PT schools also slowed; in some instances, prospective physical therapists were told at that time to not pursue a career as a physical therapist."
14. Although not of the significance of Medicare in driving demand for services, other federal and state agencies can affect demand for physical therapists and specialists within the field. For example, according to one interviewee, the DOE has rules that you must be qualified (have a master's degree or higher) to provide physical therapy services in schools and receive reimbursement.

5
Home Health and
Personal Care Aides

We selected home health aides and personal care aides for a case study because there have been many reports in the media and academic literature about shortages in the field. The labor market for this profession is interesting for several reasons. Because it is a low-skill occupation, one might expect that wages could be increased in the event of a shortage and potential entrants could enter the field rapidly. However, a key factor in the labor market for health occupations is the high degree of regulation of health care in the United States, which can prevent the labor market from freely adjusting, and this holds true for home health aides and personal care aides.

The aging of the U.S. population has been cited as a primary reason behind the demand for home health care services, and with a surge of baby boomers moving into their 50s and 60s, the need for home care services is anticipated to continue to escalate over the next two decades. Although a shortage of home care workers could result from rapidly increasing demand, other reasons to explore this occupation include the policies of various third-party insurance payers, such as the federal government, state governments, and insurance companies. Such policies, particularly with respect to reimbursement for services, can substantially affect wage rates within the home health field (which, in turn, can affect willingness of workers to enter and stay in the field). Additionally, there has been much focus on the difficulties in attracting and retaining workers in this field. Rates of attrition (especially among new workers) are often attributed to low pay, difficulties in piecing together full-time work over an extended period (across several patients), burnout, the need for reliable transportation, and a willingness to commute. The supply of workers into the field can be substantially affected by overall labor market conditions (i.e., availability of jobs in other low-wage sectors), immigration, and state policies with regard to families or friends providing care.

BACKGROUND AND DESCRIPTION

The Standard Occupational Classification (SOC) system includes two related occupations that provide paraprofessional home care services, home health aides and personal care aides. Home health aides are generally more skilled than personal care aides, and the distinctions between the occupations are discussed below.[1]

The primary duty of home health aides is to help elderly and disabled people live in their homes rather than in health care facilities. Health care aides provide health-related services, such as giving the patient medications under the direction of nursing or medical staff. Home health aides may perform a number of activities, including checking the patient's pulse rate, temperature, and respiration rate; helping with prescribed exercises; and helping the patient bathe, dress, and groom him- or herself. Home health aides with training and experience may also assist with medical equipment, such as with ventilators used to help a patient breathe. Many home health aides work with elderly and disabled people who need more extensive care than family or friends can provide. Other home health aides help discharged hospital patients with fairly short-term needs. Oftentimes, home health agencies have a registered nurse, physical therapist, or social worker supervise and assign specific duties to home health aides. The home health aide usually keeps records of the services performed and records each patient's progress, reporting changes in the patient's condition to his or her supervisor or the case manager (BLS 2010d).

Personal and home care aides have the same primary duty as home health aides—to assist elderly, disabled, ill, or mentally disabled individuals live in their own homes or in residential care facilities rather than in health facilities or institutions. However, personal and home care aides mainly provide housekeeping and routine personal care services rather than health-related services. One interviewee for this study drew the following distinction between home health workers and home care aides:

> Home health aides and home care aides are different occupations and function in quite different markets. In part, this is because home health aides are covered by Medicare, as well as Medicaid. Because home health care is an entitlement under Medicare,

the market is more formal. There are fewer self-employed home health aides (they are more likely to be employed through nursing homes, home care agencies, etc.), and this occupation requires more formal training and has certification requirements.

Personal and home care aides are sometimes called homemakers, caregivers, companions, or personal attendants. Personal and home care aides often clean clients' houses, do laundry, change bed linens, cook, run errands, and help the client bathe, groom, dress, and get in and out of bed. Personal and home care aides provide instruction and psychological support to their patients and may advise the patient's family members on nutrition, cleanliness, and household tasks. Personal and home care aides may also work for a home health agency, where a registered nurse, physical therapist, or social worker provides assignments and supervision, and the aide records the patient's progress, providing updates to the supervisor or case manager (BLS 2010d).

The establishment of Medicare and Medicaid under the Social Security Act Amendments of 1965 brought regulations for home care services as well as reimbursement mechanisms. Medicare is the federal health insurance program for Americans aged 65 or older, regardless of their income or medical history. Most people aged 65 and older are entitled to Medicare Part A (which covers hospital services) if they or their spouse are eligible for Social Security payments and have made payroll tax contributions for 10 or more years. In 1972, Medicare was expanded to include some disabled people under the age of 65 with permanent disabilities and end-stage renal (kidney) disease. Medicare Part A covers inpatient services provided by hospitals, skilled nursing facilities, hospice care, and home health services; it accounted for 36 percent of Medicare benefit spending in 2009. Medicare Part B, the supplementary medical insurance, covers physician, outpatient, preventive services, and home health visits, and accounted for 29 percent of benefit spending in 2009 (Kaiser Family Foundation 2010b).

Originally, Medicare Part A covered home health agency services after a period of hospitalization and required no cost sharing, whereas Part B covered home health agency services and required beneficiaries to meet an annual deductible. The initial legislation in 1965 included a number of qualifications that beneficiaries had to meet to receive home care services under Medicare and limited the number of days service could be provided. The Omnibus Budget Reconciliation Act of

1980 reduced barriers to the use of home health services by eliminating the 100-day visit limit, the requirement for a prior hospital stay of three days, the Part B deductible, and the requirement for proprietary agencies to be licensed by the state. In addition, the Omnibus Budget Reconciliation Act of 1987 instituted competency exams and training requirements for home health aides employed by Medicare-certified home health agencies. The specific education and training requirements for home health aides are discussed later in the "Educational Qualifications and Entry Requirements" subsection on p. 140.

In 2007, Medicare accounted for 41 percent of total national personal health expenditures on home health care services in the United States—$24 billion of a total of $59 billion expended on home health care services (Kaiser Family Foundation 2009). Medicare covers home health care under the following conditions:

- The doctor determines that medical care at home is needed.
- The person needs intermittent skilled nursing care, physical therapy, speech-language pathology services, or continued occupational therapy.
- The home health agency is Medicare-certified.
- The person is homebound or normally unable to leave home unassisted.

If a recipient is eligible for home health care, Medicare will cover home health aide services on a part-time or intermittent basis, which includes help with personal care, such as bathing, using the toilet, or dressing. Medicare will not cover home health aide services unless the recipient is also getting skilled care such as nursing care or other therapy from a home health agency. In addition, the home health aide services must be part of the care for the recipient's injury or illness. Medicare does not cover 24-hour-a-day care, meal delivery, or homemaker services, such as shopping, cleaning, and laundry (DHHS 2007b).

The CMS administers the Medicare program and certifies home health agencies by using the Institute of Medicine's definition of quality care, which includes effectiveness, efficiency, equity, patient centeredness, safety, and timeliness. The quality of care is measured by the Outcome and Assessment Information Set (OASIS), which currently gathers information on 41 home health quality measures, such as

improvements in bathing, transferring, and management of oral medication. In 2010, there were over 10,800 Medicare-certified home health
agencies throughout the United States. That year, more than 3.4 million
Medicare beneficiaries were served by home health agencies, which
made over 122 million visits (DHHS 2011).

The original intent of Medicaid was to assist elderly poor Americans in covering health care costs that Medicare did not address. The
Medicaid program was later expanded to include many low-income
families unable to afford health care through the private health care system. Medicaid eligibility is extended to two main groups, the categorically needy and the medically needy. Included among the categorically
needy are Supplemental Security Income (SSI) recipients and families who meet eligibility requirements for their states' TANF program.
Those eligible for Medicaid also include the elderly who qualify for
Medicare but cannot afford the Part A hospital deductible or the Part B
premium; these make up about 25 percent of Medicare recipients. Disabled people, pregnant women, and children from low-income families
also qualify for Medicaid. In 2007, Medicaid provided health insurance
coverage for 58 million beneficiaries, including 6 million seniors, 8.8
million persons with disabilities (including 4 million children), 29 million children, and 15 million adults (primarily poor working parents).
In 2008, home health care and personal care accounted for 14.1 percent
of overall Medicaid expenditures, totaling $339 billion (Kaiser Family
Foundation 2010c).

The Social Security Act authorizes many waivers and demonstration programs, and this gives states flexibility in designing their Medicaid programs, including a waiver program for community-based care
that has been available since 1981. The CMS Home and Community-
Based Services (HCBS) Waiver allows long-term care services to be
provided in a community setting as an alternative to institutional settings. Federal requirements for states choosing to implement an HCBS
waiver program include the following: demonstrating that providing
waiver services to a target population is no more costly than the cost
of services these individuals would receive in an institution, ensuring
that measures will be taken to protect the health and welfare of consumers, providing adequate and reasonable provider standards to meet the
needs of the target population, and ensuring that services are provided
in accordance with a plan of care.

The original intent of community-based services was to reduce the costs of health care services under Medicaid, but the program has greatly expanded since the U.S. Supreme Court case *Olmstead v. L.C.* in 1999. In 2006, 48 states (excluding Arizona and Vermont) and the District of Columbia offered services under 269 HCBS waivers; however, who is eligible and what services are covered vary from state to state (Kaiser Commission on Medicaid and the Uninsured 2009).

The Olmstead decision has been very important in expanding the option of community-based care to people with disabilities. The Olmstead case called into question whether or not unnecessary institutionalization of those with disabilities constitutes discrimination and the steps states should take to integrate people with disabilities into society. Based on this decision, many other individuals have followed suit, claiming violations of the Americans with Disabilities Act. The Olmstead decision has resulted in an expansion of community-based care efforts and motions by states to incorporate such care into their health programs.

TRAINING AND RECRUITMENT OF WORKERS

This section discusses the educational requirements and qualifications for home health and personal care aides, the factors affecting those requirements, and the employment characteristics of home health and personal care aides. This examination of the means by which individuals enter the occupation lays the groundwork for the analysis later in the chapter.

Educational Qualifications and Entry Requirements

Specific education and training requirements for home care workers vary by state and work setting. A high school diploma is required for many health aide positions, such as nursing and psychiatric aides, but a high school diploma is generally not required for jobs as home care workers. Some states only require on-the-job training, which is usually provided by the employer. Registered nurses, licensed practical nurses, or experienced aides may provide on-the-job training, or employers may provide classroom instruction for newly hired aides. Training includes instruction on how to properly cook for a client, including information on nutrition and special diets, and basic housekeeping tasks, such as keeping the home safe and sanitary for the patient. Aides are usually taught how to respond to an emergency situation and basic safety techniques. An aide may also be required to take a competency examination to ensure that he or she can perform the required tasks. Some states require formal training, which is typically offered at community colleges, vocational schools, elder care programs, and home health care agencies. A physical examination, including state-regulated tests such as those for tuberculosis, may be required. A criminal background check, credit check, and good driving record may also be required because aides are generally responsible for their own transportation and work in people's homes (BLS 2010d).

As discussed, the federal government has issued guidelines for employers of home health aides that receive reimbursement from Medicare. The Omnibus Budget Reconciliation Act of 1987 established qualifications for home health care aides who provide services for Medicare-certified home health agencies. As of August 14, 1990, certified agencies cannot use home health aides for Medicare patients unless the individual completes a training program and competency evaluation program or passes a competency evaluation program without training, demonstrating that the individual is competent to deliver home health services. The training and competency evaluation programs must meet the minimum standards established by the DHHS as outlined in 42 CFR 484.36. Training is to be a minimum of 75 hours, with at least 16 hours of classroom training, followed by at least 16 hours of supervised practical skills.

The 75-hour standard was adopted by the Health Care Financing Administration (now the CMS) to reflect the statutory requirements for nurse aides in Medicare- and Medicaid-certified nursing facilities. Federal regulations also specify requirements for instructors and training content. The training must cover 12 specific items, mostly health-related, that the CMS developed based on a model curriculum of the Foundation for Hospice and Homecare. In addition, home health agencies must conduct performance evaluations of each home health care aide at least once a year and provide at least three hours of in-service training each calendar quarter. Home health agencies are required to maintain documentation for their employees showing that the training and competency requirements of the home health aides are met. States may also have their own specific requirements for home health agencies to receive reimbursements.

The National Association for Home Care and Hospice (NAHC) has also offered voluntary certification for home health and personal care aides since 1990. Certification of an aide by NAHC is a demonstration that the aide has met industry standards. NAHC certification requires the completion of a 75-hour course; observation and documentation of 17 skills for competency, assessed by a registered nurse; and passage of a written exam (National Association for Home Care and Hospice 2009).

Methods Employers Use to Recruit Workers and Workers Use to Obtain Employment

Word of mouth is among the most frequently used methods that home care workers employ to find jobs. For example, home care workers often hear about job openings from other home care workers, as well as informally through talking and networking with families and friends. Home care workers also increasingly look on the Web sites of home care agencies to see if they have vacancies, or they may directly contact such providers and inquire about job openings. Those interested in becoming home health aides or home care attendants may first volunteer at a local nursing home, hospice, or hospital to gain experience and contacts (and to gauge their interest in entering the field). New entrants to the field, who may have completed a certified nursing assistant program or another caregiver program, may hear about openings from other trainees, instructors, or administrators. Community colleges and proprietary schools typically have placement offices to help graduates find employment and often receive job listings from larger employers in their localities.

Home care workers may also use more general approaches—scanning newspaper advertisements for openings, using employment Web sites with job listings, or looking for job openings in listings maintained at public employment service offices or other staffing agencies. Over the past decade, the ability to search for job openings over the Internet (through search engines and by accessing Web sites for specific employers hiring large numbers of home care workers) has become an increasingly important way in which workers look for and secure jobs in the industry. Other ways in which workers may learn about job openings are through advertisements on the radio, television, buses, and subways; attending meetings (and networking) at community groups and churches; and looking at job listings or meeting with staff/case managers at welfare offices and other community-based organizations. Workers also may attend job fairs sponsored by public employment agencies or associations of health care providers.

Employers use many of these same procedures to attract workers—listing job openings on their Web sites or on more generalized employment Web sites, listing openings with public employment agencies and staffing agencies, and advertising through various media. They also may rely to some extent on their existing workforce to do outreach and recruit family, relatives, friends, and acquaintances. With some states such as California adopting consumer-directed initiatives, consumers are increasingly involved in identifying and recruiting individuals (often family members or friends) to serve as caregivers.

CHARACTERISTICS OF WORKERS

Home Health Aides

By May 2010, about one-third (342,500 workers) of the total 982,840 home health aides employed in the United States worked for home health care services agencies. The second-largest setting for home health aides was residential facilities for the mentally disabled, accounting for about 19 percent of home health aide employment (188,440 workers), followed by individual and family services, accounting for 15 percent (148,190 workers), and community care facilities for the elderly, accounting for 14 percent (142,090 workers). Only 4 percent of home health aides (about 43,660 workers) worked in nursing care facilities, and 7 percent of all home health aides were self-employed (BLS 2010d).

According to the National Health Statistics Report *An Overview of Home Health Aides* (Bercovitz et al. 2011), approximately one-half of home care workers were at least 35 years of age in 2007, with the vast majority of home health aides being female (according to the 2000 census, only 8 percent of home care workers were male); approximately one-half were white and one-third were black. In the 2000 census, 57 percent of home care workers were white, 28 percent were black, and 8 percent were Hispanic or Latino (additionally, 15 percent of home care workers spoke a language other than English at home, and about 12 percent of home care workers were foreign-born). The 2000 census also reported that only about one-third (34.3 percent) of U.S. home care workers worked full time year-round. This points to the often part-time nature of home care work and, together with the relatively low wage levels (discussed in the next section), suggests that total earnings for home care workers on an annual basis are low. In 2007, two-thirds of home health aides had an annual family income of less than $40,000 (Bercovitz et al. 2011).

Personal Care Aides

According to 2010 figures, while home health care service agencies are the largest employer of home health aides, only 26 percent of personal care aides work for home health care service agencies, whereas 33 percent of the workforce provides services for the elderly and persons with disabilities. The third-largest setting for personal care aides is private households, accounting for 10 percent, and the fourth is vocational rehabilitation services, accounting for nearly 5 percent (BLS 2010d). The 2000 census reported that 96 percent of all home care workers did not have a college degree, 29 percent had less than a high school education, 38 percent were high school graduates only, and 30 percent had achieved some college education (Montgomery et al. 2005).

EMPLOYMENT AND EARNINGS TRENDS

Employment Trends

Employment levels and change

Table 5.1 shows the trends in the number of home health and personal and home care aides compared to health care support occupations, personal care and service occupations, and all workers from 2006 to

Table 5.1 Number of and Percentage Change for Home Health and Personal Care Aides, Comparison Occupations, and All Workers, 2006–2010

Occupation	2006	2007	2008	2009	2010	% change
Home health aides	751,480	834,580	892,410	955,220	982,840	30.8
Nursing aides, orderlies, and attendants	1,376,660	1,390,260	1,422,720	1,438,010	1,451,090	5.4
Psychiatric aides	57,000	58,310	59,050	62,610	64,730	13.6
All health care support occupations	3,483,270	3,625,240	3,779,280	3,886,690	3,962,930	13.8
Personal and home care aides	578,290	595,350	614,190	630,740	686,030	18.6
Child care workers	572,950	576,680	581,670	595,650	611,280	6.7
All personal care and service occupations	3,249,760	3,339,510	3,437,520	3,461,910	3,425,220	5.4
All workers from all occupations	132,604,980	134,354,250	135,185,230	130,647,610	127,097,160	−4.2

SOURCE: 2006–2009 data: BLS (2011a); 2010 data: BLS (2011b).

2010. As the table shows, the number of home health aides and personal and home care aides increased every year over this five-year period, increasing by a total of 30.8 percent, which is much higher than the rate for all workers (–4.2 percent) and for all health care support workers (13.8 percent) over the same time period. From 2006 to 2010, the number of personal and home care aides increased by 18.6 percent, which is also higher than all of the comparison occupations, except for home health aides. The addition of more than 231,000 home health aides (a 30 percent increase) over the past five years is indicative of a strong demand for workers within the field. As discussed later in this chapter, rapid growth in the number of workers within the home health care field is a reflection of expanding demand for services (e.g., as the U.S. population ages and many more older individuals require such services) and availability of resources from Medicare, Medicaid, and other third-party payers to reimburse recipients for the cost of home health care services.

Unemployment trends

Another key indicator of labor market conditions for a given occupation is the annual average unemployment rate. Occupations experiencing tight labor market conditions, in which the number of vacancies is greater than the number of qualified applicants, are likely to have very low unemployment rates because those searching for jobs find them quickly and are unemployed for a very short period. There are, however, exceptions to this trend, particularly in occupations with high turnover. Table 5.2 illustrates the trend in the annual unemployment rate for home health aides, personal and home care aides, comparison occupations, and all workers from all occupations; however, in the table the BLS groups home health aides with nursing and psychiatric aides when calculating unemployment rates. The annual unemployment rate for personal and home care aides averaged 7.9 percent between 2006 and 2010, compared to 6.5 percent for nursing, psychiatric, and home health aides, and 6.2 percent for all workers from all occupations. Over the past five years, the unemployment rates for personal and home care aides and nursing, psychiatric, and home health aides have followed a similar year-to-year path and fluctuated in roughly a similar percentage range, with the rate for personal and home care aides ranging from 5.9

Table 5.2 Average Annual Unemployment Rate (%) for Home Health Aides and Personal and Home Care Aides, Comparison Occupations, and All Workers, 2006–2010

Occupation	2006	2007	2008	2009	2010
Nursing, psychiatric, and home health aides	5.6	5.2	5.2	7.4	9.2
Physical therapist assistants and aides	0.6	0.4	3.2	6.3	3.5
All health care support occupations	4.6	4.5	4.5	6.8	7.6
Personal and home care aides	6.4	5.9	7.1	9.9	10.1
Child care workers	5.7	6.2	7.4	9.1	10.5
All personal care and service occupations	4.7	4.8	5.7	8.0	8.7
All workers from all occupations	4.2	4.2	5.3	8.6	8.9

SOURCE: Unpublished BLS data from the Current Population Survey (2006–2010), Table 3: Annual average employed and experienced unemployed persons by detailed occupation and class of worker.

to 10.1 percent and the range for nursing, psychiatric, and home health aides ranging from 5.2 to 9.2 percent.

By 2010, the unemployment rates for home health aides and personal and home care aides were slightly higher than the unemployment rate for all workers from all occupations. The relatively high unemployment rates for home care workers do not (at least on the surface) suggest a tight labor market condition or shortage. As discussed below, because of a variety of factors (e.g., low wages, sometimes difficult working conditions and long commutes, turnover of patients, burnout, and a variety of other factors), there are high rates of attrition and much churning of workers within the home care sector (potentially explaining the high unemployment rates for these workers). Interviewees for this study, knowledgeable about the home care industry and employment patterns, were all in agreement about the high levels of turnover among workers in the sector, particularly among those newly entering the profession. This constant turnover might explain why employers (e.g., home care agencies) on the one hand indicated that they have almost constant job vacancies that they have difficulty filling, yet unemployment rates within the occupation remain above average (indicating a sizable potential pool for filling vacancies within the occupation).

Projections for future employment growth

Although employment growth in home health and home care aides has been rapid in recent years, in the future the field is anticipated to see even further growth (Table 5.3). The BLS estimates that, between the years 2010 and 2018, the total number of home health aides will increase by 40.7 percent, compared to estimated increases of 20.3 percent for nursing aides, orderlies, and attendants and 2.1 percent for psychiatric aides. In addition, the increase in home health worker employment is expected to exceed the increase for all workers in all occupations, estimated at about 30.8 percent for this time period. Others have projected trends beyond the next decade and suggested that employment in the home care industry will continue to grow through at least the middle of the century because of demographic trends. For example, the DHHS (2003) has projected high continued growth for direct care workers in long-term care settings primarily because of demographic trends. According to estimates developed by DHHS's Office of the Assistant Secretary for Planning and Evaluation (ASPE), the demand for direct care workers in long-term care settings becomes even greater as the baby boomers reach age 85, beginning in 2030. ASPE projects the demand for direct care workers to grow to approximately 5.7 to 6.6 million workers in 2050. This increase in demand will be occurring at a

Table 5.3 Employment Projections for Home Health Aides, Comparison Occupations, and All Workers, 2010 and 2018 (projected)

Occupation	2010	Projected 2018	% change
Home health aides	982,840	1,382,600	40.7
Personal and home care aides	686,030	1,193,000	73.9
Nursing aides, orderlies, and attendants	1,451,090	1,745,800	20.3
Psychiatric aides	64,730	66,100	2.1
All workers from all occupations	127,097,160	166,206,000	30.8

SOURCE: BLS (2010d, 2011b).

time when the supply of workers who have traditionally filled these jobs is expected to increase only slightly. These projections indicate that it is critical to retain existing long-term care workers and attract new ones. Since many industries will be competing for the supply of workers, pay and working conditions will play a key role in attracting new workers and consequently in influencing the supply of long-term care services.

The interviewees for this study all agreed that employment growth would be robust in the field, pointing to the inevitability of demographics (the aging population) driving demand. For example, according to one interviewee,

> Our organization relies on the concept of "care gap"—the gap between demand for workers and supply. In the past, our organization did this in a crude (proxy) way, looking at the number of women expected to enter workforce aged 25–55 and comparing this to what is known about expected demand for home care workers (using occupational projections from the BLS). This type of analysis reveals a long-term challenge—you see a trickle of women coming into the workforce in the relevant age group compared to the future demand for services as the population ages (and medical technology keeps people living longer). For example, in upstate New York there is a shrinking number of workers going into the workforce and yet increasing demand for home care services.

Earnings Trends

The relative wage rate change in an occupation is often an important indicator of labor market dynamics, especially in the short run. In occupations where market forces move freely, a rapid rise in wages may indicate the presence of a shortage. Although home care workers have seen a consistent increase in median hourly wages from 2006 to 2010 (as shown in Table 5.4), home health aides have only seen a 5.9 percent increase in median wages over those five years (from $9.34 in 2006 to $9.89 in 2010). Personal and home care aides experienced a larger increase over the five-year period (10.5 percent, from $8.54 in 2006 to $9.44 in 2010), although this is still slightly less than the 11.4 percent increase in median wages that all workers from all occupations experienced during the same period.

Table 5.4 Median Hourly Earnings ($) and Percentage Change for Home Health Aides, Personal and Home Care Aides, Comparison Occupations, and All Workers, 2006–2010

Occupation	2006	2007	2008	2009	2010	% change
Home health aides	9.34	9.62	9.84	9.85	9.89	5.9
Nursing aides, orderlies, and attendants	10.67	11.14	11.46	11.56	11.54	8.2
Psychiatric aides	11.49	12.25	12.77	12.33	12.00	4.4
All health care support occupations	11.00	11.45	11.80	11.89	11.90	8.2
Personal and home care aides	8.54	8.89	9.22	9.46	9.44	10.5
Child care workers	8.48	8.82	9.12	9.25	9.28	9.4
All personal care and service occupations	9.17	9.50	9.82	9.99	9.92	8.2
All workers from all occupations	14.61	15.10	15.57	15.95	16.27	11.4

SOURCE: BLS (2011c).

The experts interviewed for this study as well as the literature all note that the relatively low wage rates for home care workers are a critical factor both in terms of recruitment of new workers into the field and, once they are in the field, of retaining those workers. As discussed later in this chapter, public sector programs—in particular, the Medicare and Medicaid programs—reimburse home care providers for a large portion of home care services. As a result, the government sector, in conjunction with health insurers, is largely responsible for setting wage levels within the industry, including for home care workers. With wages set at relatively low levels, it is not unusual for employers (and analysts) to observe that home care providers are in competition with fast food restaurants and other low-wage industry sectors for workers. For example, several of the interviewees for this study identified low pay (accompanied by a general lack of other fringe benefits) as hampering recruitment of new workers into the field and contributing to the loss of existing workers into other low-wage jobs, including this interviewee:

> Low pay (resulting from low reimbursement rates from states), inconsistent hours, and poor quality job conditions lead to turnover and make it difficult to attract and keep workers in the profession. About 40 percent of home care workers need public assistance (food stamps, TANF, Medicaid) to subsist because of poor pay and benefits. A major factor in shortages [is formed by] public policies that do not encourage better pay/benefits, better training, and supervision done in a way that [makes] home care workers want to stay in their jobs.

LABOR MARKET FACTORS CONTRIBUTING TO A SHORTAGE

Demand-Side Factors

Aging of the population

One of the most prominent factors cited in the literature (and in interviews conducted for this study) with respect to current and future concerns about potential shortfalls of home health aides and home care workers is the aging of the U.S. population. The older population, those 65 years or older, has grown substantially in recent years and is expected to grow rapidly over the next quarter of a century. In 2009, the most recent date for which data are available, there were an estimated 39.6 million elderly people, which is a 15.1 percent increase from 1998, when there were 34.4 million elderly Americans. Whereas in 2000 the elderly (aged 65 and over) population represented 12.4 percent of the total population, by 2030 this age bracket is expected to grow to 19.0 percent of the total population. In addition, 5.7 million Americans were over the age of 85 in 2008, and this number is projected to grow to 6.6 million in 2020. In 2009, older Americans (those over 65 years of age) comprised 12.9 percent of the U.S. population, which is equivalent to nearly one in every eight Americans (DHHS 2010). In addition, about 30.5 percent or 11.2 million noninstitutionalized older people lived alone in 2008.

A majority of Americans aged 65 or older have at least one chronic health condition. Highlighting this point, in 2009, 41.6 percent of noninstitutionalized older persons assessed their health as excellent or very good (compared to 64.5 percent for all persons aged 18–64 years). From 2006 to 2008, the most common chronic conditions were diagnosed arthritis (50 percent), hypertension (38 percent), all types of heart disease (32 percent), any cancer (22 percent), diabetes (18 percent), and sinusitis (14 percent). In addition, chronic conditions and disabilities increase with age; for example, 56 percent of people over 80 years of age reported a severe disability, and 29 percent of people over 80 reported they needed assistance (DHHS 2010). The recent and expected growth in the proportion of older Americans is significant because older people tend to need and spend more on health care and, in particular, are much more likely to require home health and other home care services than younger individuals.

As discussed earlier, Medicare is the public insurance program for Americans over the age of 65. In 2009, almost all (93.5 percent) noninstitutionalized persons aged 65 and over were covered by Medicare. In addition, in 2009, about 9 percent of the noninstitutionalized elderly were covered by Medicaid. Among Medicare beneficiaries, over 25 percent of those living in the community had difficulty performing one or more activities of daily living (ADLs), and an additional 14.6 percent reported difficulties with instrumental activities of daily living (IADLs) (DHHS 2010).[2] As a result, about 11 percent or 3.7 million older Medicare enrollees received personal care in 1999. Nearly all older people (91 percent) living in the community with chronic conditions received either informal care from family or a combination of formal and informal care. Nine percent of the chronically disabled elderly received only formal care from home health care aides in 1999 (DHHS 2008a). Hence, with the surge of baby boomers moving into their 50s and 60s, it is projected that demand for home care services will continue to build until at least the middle of the century.

Expansion of publicly funded home care services

As discussed earlier, there have been several legislative changes over the years that have expanded eligibility and services for home care covered by Medicare and Medicaid. The increasing availability of insurance—Medicare, Medicaid, and private insurance—to cover the cost of home health care services has made it possible for many older and infirm individuals to obtain home care services that might have otherwise been provided in an institutional setting (or by family members or not at all). The number of Medicare-certified home health care agencies, the major employers of home care workers, has steadily grown to meet demand for services: between 2001 and 2009, there was a 54 percent increase in the number of certified agencies, from 6,861 to 10,581 (National Association for Home Care and Hospice 2010).

Similar to Medicare, Medicaid spending on home care services has also been on the rise. Medicaid spending on home care more than doubled between 2000 and 2007 ($22.5 billion in 2000 to $55.9 billion in 2007), illustrating how states have begun to place a greater emphasis on providing home care. Additionally, the CMS estimated that Americans spent a total of $65 billion for home care services in 2008 (National Association for Home Care and Hospice 2010). In 2000, Medicaid expenditures represented 30 percent of total long-term care expenditures. By 2006, Medicaid accounted for 40 percent of the nearly $178 billion spent on long-term care services. Spending patterns for Medicaid home and community-based services varies by state, but demand for these services is evidenced by the number of beneficiaries on waiting lists for home and community-based waiver services. In 2008, about 393,096 beneficiaries were on waiting lists for home care services in 38 states, which is an 18.5 percent increase from 2007 (Kaiser Family

Foundation 2010b). Both Medicare and Medicaid have seen an increase in demand for home care services from their beneficiaries,[3] which is likely a result of the increase in home care options available from these public programs, as discussed earlier in the chapter.[4] Both the literature and interviewees identified changes in public policies under Medicare and Medicaid on reimbursement for home health care services as key factors in the steady growth of demand for such services. Several interviewees pointed to the great importance of Medicare and Medicaid in shaping trends in the long-term sector (and escalating the demand for workers to provide such services). For example, one interviewee observed that changes in Medicaid policies had had a profound effect on demand for home health care services dating back to over a quarter century ago:

> Such shortages (i.e., for home health care workers) probably date back to 1975 when home care became an option under Medicaid. In 1975, states were given the option of covering personal care assistants. This greatly increased demand for home care workers. In 1981 waiver authority gave states the right to waive some Medicaid rules to cover all categories of Medicaid recipients for LTC [long-term care] (e.g., women with infant children, SSI recipients, etc.). This led to waivers in all states that usually expanded demand for home care and enabled states to deinstitutionalize many people from state hospitals and intermediate care facilities (ICFs).

More recently, states such as California and Vermont have initiated consumer-directed initiatives under their Medicaid programs, and these initiatives have substantially altered the ways in which patients in need of home care services recruit caregivers and, according to one interviewee, have further induced demand for home care services:

> There are about 440,000 consumers receiving home care services in California and 120,000 home care workers visiting homes (95 percent paid by Medicaid). Providers are independent providers (hired/fired/supervised by consumer). This means that the consumer is almost always hiring someone they know—about half hire family members. Formal provision of long-term care is very intertwined with informal care in the state. There is a lot of informal care—the demand for formal care is defined by the number of hours authorized to provide care—but authorized hours are often inadequate and so informal care needs to fill in where formal care

falls short. Many times the formal and informal care person is the same, so the informal care person fills in the gaps in care. In effect, this hides the extent of the labor shortage. Overall, the consumer-directed system used in California induces demand for paid care.

Supply-Side Factors

Low pay and inadequate fringe benefits make recruitment and retention challenging

Much past research on the labor market conditions for home care workers has pointed to relatively low wage levels and the lack of fringe benefits as perhaps the greatest barriers to entry and compounding factors when it comes to keeping workers within the field of home care. As discussed below, low wages together with often-difficult working conditions are among the key factors that lead to burnout and high rates of turnover within the field. Interviewees were in agreement that low wage rates and fringe benefits tempered the enthusiasm of even the most highly motivated to enter and stay in the field of home health care. The median hourly wage for home health aides was $9.89 in 2010 (Table 5.4), an hourly wage not much above what workers might make as cashiers, working in fast food restaurants, or at other low-paying service sector jobs. In fact, those working in the field often come from (and later leave to take) other low-paying service sector jobs, often moving to jobs with less stress, regular hours, and lower levels of commuting. Interviewees noted that current wage levels of home care workers, together with difficulties in consistently putting together full-time hours (generally across several patients), meant that workers in the field may have to rely on food stamps and other assistance to make ends meet.

Like many other low-paying jobs, fringe benefits for workers within the field of home health care can be meager, leaving workers (ironically) to fend for themselves when it comes to securing health insurance (even as they provide health care services for their insured patients). Figure 5.1 displays the types of fringe benefits home care agencies offer to caregivers. Slightly over half (56 percent) offer aides paid time off, and slightly less than half (48 percent) offer health insurance. Other types of benefits are even less frequently offered to home

Figure 5.1   Percentage of Home Health Agencies Offering Various Types of Health Benefits to Home Health Aides, 2008

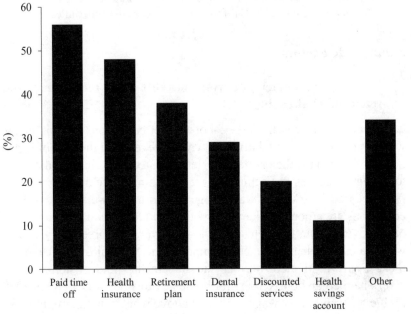

SOURCE: National Private Duty Association (2008).

health aides, such as retirement plans (38 percent), dental insurance (29 percent), and health saving accounts (11 percent).

Difficult working conditions, low pay, and inadequate benefits lead to high turnover and attrition

Difficult working conditions, including inadequate training, heavy workloads, few tangible rewards for performance, and little or no supportive supervision, also contribute to the difficulties with recruitment and turnover (Benjamin et al. 2008). These challenging working conditions are often further exacerbated by staff vacancies (due to high turnover) and the lack of a backup workforce. In addition, home health workers face other occupational hazards, including violence in neighborhoods and homes, lack of workstations, heavy patient lifting, improper disposal of dressings or sharp medical devices, and high productivity demands (Markkaned et al. 2007). The need for reliable transportation and a willingness to drive considerable distances to provide services (particularly in rural areas) are often requirements of being a home care worker. For example, a study found that health care workers drove nearly 5 billion miles to serve nearly 12 million elderly and disabled patients in the United States in 2006. Because of the recent increases in gas prices, many home health care providers have stopped providing service to remote areas, reduced their service areas, and lost home care workers who cannot afford the higher commuting costs (Foundation for Hospice and Homecare 2006).

Both the literature and our interviews with experts indicate that poor pay and fringe benefits, combined with challenging working conditions, are key factors in the high turnover rates within the home care field. A recent survey of home health agencies in New Hampshire found that turnover was not a problem in only 13 percent of the agencies surveyed, with 35 percent of respondents reporting turnover to be a somewhat serious or serious problem (Smith 2009). In a 2005 survey of the literature, Wright (2005) found many studies indicating very high turnover among home care workers and other direct care workers; for example, in one study, 35 of 44 states surveyed indicated that turnover was a serious issue in their state, and estimates of turnover in specific studies were often in the 25 to 50 percent range. Frequent turnover and the lack of a sufficient number of home health aides and personal care workers may also result in poor quality of care for patients, disruptions in continuity of care, reduced access to care, increased pressure on family caregivers, or increased rates of injuries or accidents (Stone 2004).

Interviewees for this study were in agreement that high rates of turnover, especially among new entrants and younger home care workers, was a particular challenge afflicting the home care industry—one that has led to much churning and at the very least a perception on the part of home care agencies that they needed to be on the constant lookout for qualified new entrants to fill vacant home care positions. According to one interviewee, there are a number of factors (including general economic conditions) that are responsible for high turnover rates in the occupation:

> We see a lot of turnover and movement in the sector—when the economy gets more robust, people are looking to get paid more and leave the field. We have found in interviews with home care

workers that they see their profession as a caring one (also, their
life is their own, they have little supervision, and work in homes).
Many prefer to work in a home care setting to nursing homes, but
the pay is not as much, getting enough hours can be a problem, and
travel can be an issue.

A second interviewee viewed wage levels as a critical determinant
of turnover rates within a particular locality:

Turnover is related to wages paid—we have found that turnover
drops significantly for new entrants if wage rates are 20 percent
above the tenth decile of income in a locality . . . In California,
you see turnover is lower in counties where there have been wage
increases; and more importantly, where health insurance has been
offered of a certain scale. You are most likely to see shortages in
low-wage urban areas where there have not been wage increases
and rural areas where wages hover around minimum wage.

Other potential supply factors

Interviewees indicated that at the same time that the U.S. population is aging, there is a demographic factor that is a drag on the supply
of new workers to the home care field: women between the ages of 25
and 45—the primary population group that has traditionally provided
home care services—is not growing. Additional opportunities within
and outside of the health care field have also opened up to women who
may have in the past taken jobs in the home care field. Several interviewees also pointed to the apparent increasing difficulty of bringing
young workers into the field of home care, as well as very high rates of
attrition from the field during the initial three months after entry.

General labor market conditions, according to study interviewees,
can also play an important role in the overall supply of available (low-
wage) workers and their willingness to take home care jobs. When economic conditions are good, and there are other better or similar paying opportunities available, home health agencies may encounter much
greater difficulties in filling vacant home care positions. For example,
according to one interviewee, there has been considerable flux in general labor market conditions affecting the hiring prospects of home care
providers:

Anecdotally, home care workers are staying longer in jobs than in
the past because it is hard to get a job. The labor market changes

over time. In the late 1980s, there was a significant shortage (of home care workers); in the early 2000s, there was a workforce crisis in terms of workers . . . The recession has made it less of a problem. Right now, it is not clear if there is a shortage—the recession has had such an impact on labor market conditions. Shortages are always more of a problem in good (economic) times.

ASSESSMENT OF LABOR MARKET/ SHORTAGE CONDITIONS

Typically, dynamic labor markets tend to respond to a mismatch between supply and demand by improving wages, benefits, and working conditions. However, the home health worker labor market faces the additional constraint of third-party payers, especially publicly funded home health care services. As discussed earlier, Medicare and Medicaid account for well over half the reimbursement for long-term care services provided in the United States. In having such a dominant share of the total market for home care services, these two programs play a key role in determining reimbursement levels and restrict the flexibility of home care agencies to change wage levels in response to labor market conditions. Medicare, Medicaid, other public long-term care programs, and even private insurers to a large extent determine the amount they are willing to pay for home health care services per client, per illness, or per visit. In addition, public programs often add the extra burden of additional requirements, such as specific qualifications to provide services and the paperwork required to receive reimbursement. Therefore, third-party payers affect the flexibility of major home care agencies to increase wages, enhance benefits, and improve working conditions to attract and retain home health workers.

Because of the informalities inherent in this labor market (for example, family or friends often fill the void when limits of care are reached or when it is problematic to arrange for care), it is not easy to detect whether shortages exist. The availability of informal care to some extent masks shortages—if care for pay cannot be arranged, a family member might step in to help out (e.g., in the evening or at night), as noted by one interviewee:

> It is important whether they are family/friend or unrelated (to the patient for whom care is being provided). In California, which has a huge consumer-directed program, 80 percent of caregivers are family/friends. It is very messy in California: How do you treat a family member who is paid? Do they have to go through the same kind of training program? There is a growing group of home care workers that are family members and paid for the home care services being provided. There is also a large shadow economy of home care workers who are being paid off the books. We are totally undercounting the number of workers because we are not taking into consideration the workers providing services in this shadow economy.

Furthermore, tight labor market conditions also might be mitigated to some extent by the substitution of more costly inpatient care for services that might otherwise have been provided in a home or community setting.

There is further complication with regard to assessing shortages because, as two interviewees observed, there is a "quality" dimension to the care being provided and a perception on the part of the consumer as to the timeliness and quality of care received. With constraints on wages, home care agencies may struggle to find qualified workers that can come up to the standards expected, says one interviewee:

> Defining the characteristics of home care workers is an issue—I talk about the shortage of "good quality" home care workers—I distinguish between a warm body and a worker that is trained to perform the work (as a home care worker). We don't know exactly what quality is—that is a loaded term. It is important to draw the distinction—you can literally get a warm body, but what does that mean?

Detecting shortages within the field of home care is also complicated by the fact that with generally low wage rates being offered, the pool of workers available to fill open positions can expand and contract with general labor market conditions and with other low-wage opportunities within a given locality. The interviewees were in agreement that in good economic times the available labor force to fill home care positions to some extent dries up, as home care workers are lured from long-term care jobs into other positions and as the pool of potential new entrants to home care look to other job possibilities. On the other hand, when economic conditions deteriorate and are less than robust (as has been the case since the downturn of the U.S. economy beginning in late 2008) there is a much larger and more willing pool of low-wage workers to fill home health and home care positions.

Finally, several of the interviewees pointed not only to general economic conditions but to the "time and place" dimension of shortages (and perceived shortages)—that is, at any point in time, there may be certain localities, types of areas (e.g., rural areas), or even regions of the country where it is difficult for home care agencies to fill vacancies and for consumers in need of home care to secure such care. Several of the interviewees noted that labor markets could vary quite a bit by locality, and that varying conditions could at least in part be the result of variation across states in reimbursement policies, the structure of the home care system, and other unique circumstances. For example, one interviewee suggested that there is a great deal of variation with regard to labor market conditions across the United States at any given time:

> I think about geographic variation in terms of pockets (where it is difficult to find workers). Areas heavily hit by recession are having an easier time getting people—Ohio, West Virginia, and parts of Pennsylvania. New York City is heavily unionized and has the highest wages for home care workers, so they have fewer problems in attracting people.

A common problem in rural areas is finding home care workers willing to travel long distances between patients to provide care. Another analyst observed that the generosity of benefits and coverage can be a factor in recruiting and retaining home care workers:

> There is not a shortage of home care workers in New York City. New York City has one of the most generous long-term care programs in the country—no caps on the number of hours that can be received per month (compared to California where there is a cap of 283 hours per month). In New York City workers can make full-time jobs out of caring for a single person. Workers don't have to travel all over the city to care for a lot of people—so it is a more stable job in New York City.

Finally, a third interviewee underscored the difficulty in assessing shortages at the national level and pointed to a factor such as immigration as potentially affecting labor market conditions:

> With regard to how serious the current shortage is—it may not
> make sense to talk of the country as a whole—it probably makes
> more sense to look at regions or states. Shortages are typically less
> intense in areas where there is an influx of lower income immigrant
> population; for example, in New York City conditions are better,
> but there are tremendous shortages in upstate New York, where the
> population is shrinking and there are not new immigrants.

On balance, because wage rates are determined to a large extent by
third-party payers (principally Medicaid and Medicare), employers in
the home care sector do not enjoy the kind of flexibility that employers
in other industry sectors may have to adjust wages to boost the supply of new workers into the field (and retain existing ones). Low wage
levels, a paucity of fringe benefits, and often demanding working conditions result in substantial churning of workers within the home care
industry, and in some instances, loss of workers (especially in favorable
economic times) to other low-wage industry sectors. The literature and
experts interviewed for this study suggested that in the past there have
been periods of very tight labor markets for home care workers, and
in some regions or localities, labor market tightness has bordered on
shortages. The inability to rapidly make adjustments to wage levels and
fringe benefits and the need for home health care workers to meet certain public sector training requirements are critical factors constraining
employers from instituting changes to increase the supply of new workers and hold on to existing workers. There have been some changes and
innovations in recent years—notably a movement toward consumer-
directed recruitment of workers—to attempt to bring new workers
(especially family members and friends of patients) into the industry.

With persistently high levels of unemployment (hovering around
10 percent during much of the past two years), there does not appear to
be a current shortage of home care workers in the United States. However, it is possible that because of high rates of attrition and difficulties
in attracting workers to certain localities, there are home care agencies in some regions and localities of the country that face hardships in
terms of filling vacancies at prevailing wage levels that are fully reimbursable by third-party payers. With the aging of the U.S. population,
it is clear that strong demand for workers in this field will continue for
many years to come. What is not clear (especially given budgetary constraints and calls for fiscal austerity in public sector programs such as

Medicare and Medicaid) is whether wage rates will be able to rise fast enough to bring enough workers into the home care sector to meet surging demand for home and community-based services. The slow growth in wage levels within the occupation in recent years is not encouraging for the future.

Notes

1. For additional details about the home health aide occupation, as well as about the personal and home care aide occupation, see BLS (2010e). The background information in this section relating to the nature of the work, training and other qualifications, and outlook for future labor market conditions for this field are based in part on the discussion in this handbook.
2. ADLs include bathing, dressing, eating, and getting around the house. IADLs include preparing meals, shopping, managing money, using the telephone, doing housework, and taking medication.
3. In contrast to Medicare and Medicaid, the proportion of private funding sources (including private insurance and out-of-pocket expenses) paying for home health care services declined from 45 percent in 2000 to 21 percent in 2007.
4. Other public funding sources for home health care services include the Older Americans Act, Title XX Social Services Block Grants, the Veterans Administration, and the Civilian Health and Medical Program of the Uniformed Services.

6
Conclusions and Recommendations for Further Action

We first looked at occupational shortages nearly two decades ago (Trutko et al. 1993), and although we continue to define the economic concept of a labor shortage in the same manner, our specific findings on the presence or absence of shortages have changed over the years, and we have somewhat changed our views on how shortage data should be collected and used. It is not surprising that our findings on the existence of shortages have changed, because shortages are dependent on overall economic conditions and, in some instances, market regulation by the government or other parties, and economic conditions are quite different in 2011 than they were in 1993.[1] The much looser labor market in the current environment is likely to dampen or eliminate any occupational shortage stemming from rapidly increasing demand. It is the lack of a shortage in the economic sense that has made us realize that what Arrow and Capron (1959) called a "social demand shortage" is of more than academic interest, and this issue is highlighted in the section below.

In this concluding chapter, three major topics are addressed. First, the primary overarching findings from the case studies are provided. Next, there is a discussion of the utility of occupational shortage data for various constituencies. Finally, a discussion is presented of how better data on occupational shortages or, more generally, labor market tightness can be developed.

CONCLUSIONS FROM THE CASE STUDIES

Three overarching conclusions emerged from the case studies of the four occupations analyzed (special education teachers, pharmacists, physical therapists, and home care workers): 1) measuring occupational shortages is difficult, 2) there was no strong evidence of shortages, and

165

3) for policy purposes it is important to go beyond an economic concept of a shortage. In addition, some occupations with tight labor markets have increased educational standards in recent years.

Measuring Occupational Shortages Is Difficult

Although it is not difficult to speak conceptually about what an occupational labor shortage is, documenting that a shortage exists is quite another matter. In this project, a shortage was defined as a sustained situation where the number of workers employers would like to hire exceeds the number of workers available at the prevailing wage. There are several reasons why this definition is difficult to apply to actual labor market situations.

First, the definition requires measurement of job vacancies for specific occupations. Unfortunately, there is no national job vacancy database. The BLS has conducted the Job Openings and Labor Turnover Survey (JOLTS) since December 2000, but the number of firms included in the survey is too small to generate openings by occupation (BLS 2010e; Clark and Hyson 2001).[2] As discussed later in this chapter, vacancy data are useful for a variety of purposes, and about 15 states and roughly the same number of local areas conduct their own vacancy data surveys that do include job vacancies by occupation.[3]

Second, even if vacancy data were available, it is not a simple matter to define what constitutes a shortage. There will always be some vacancies for jobs as part of the natural labor market process. As is the case for unemployment, a certain proportion of vacancies could be considered as "frictional" and needed for the labor market to function well. Moreover, the length of time that a job is open could be an important factor in determining whether a vacancy is a sign of a shortage or simply an indication of a well-functioning labor market. Finally, just as some occupations typically have higher unemployment rates among workers in the field than other occupations, the level that is indicative of a shortage could and most likely does differ across occupations.

Third, the occupational classification system used by the U.S. government, the SOC system, does not correspond to the occupational concepts used by employers. One issue is that the SOC includes 840 detailed occupations, but employers do not necessarily define their jobs to conform to these definitions.[4] Two studies by National Research

Council (NRC) committees illustrate this problem. An NRC committee looking at the IT workforce concluded that "Definitions of occupations—which are necessarily relatively stable over time—do not necessarily reflect the IT job titles of today because new types of jobs emerge quickly. In particular, occupational categories are generally too coarse and do not reflect important distinctions among IT jobs" (National Research Council 2001, p. 278). For example, the SOC occupation "computer programmer" includes both Java and COBOL programmers, but the skills required for the two types of programming are very different, so aggregate data on all computer programmers would be of little use in assessing the computer programmer labor market. Another NRC committee examined the workforce for the National Aeronautics and Space Administration (NASA), and the committee discovered similar problems in using BLS data to analyze the labor market for NASA: "Furthermore, in the BLS classification of occupations, all aerospace engineers are grouped together, and important specialties such as systems engineering are not identified at all. NASA's job definitions do not correspond with the standard occupational classifications produced by BLS, which lack sufficient detail to be useful for NASA planning" (National Research Council 2007, p. 20).

Finally, various parties have incentives to distort the labor market situation. Employers may wish to exaggerate the tightness of the labor market if they wish to import foreign labor, whereas unions and other worker organizations may wish to minimize the extent of a shortage to avoid increases in the use of foreign labor. Although interviews can be useful in assessing whether there is a shortage, it is important to keep in mind that the people interviewed may not be objective in their assessments.

There Was No Strong Evidence of Occupational Shortages

In previous studies of occupational labor shortages, we frequently found evidence of shortages in one or more occupations, but in the current study, none of the occupations exhibited strong evidence of a shortage. In all four occupations analyzed, the labor market was fairly tight, but there was no consistent evidence that vacancies could not be filled within a reasonable amount of time. Some individuals interviewed, particularly individuals with an employer perspective, did suggest that there is currently a shortage, but they meant that there was a decline in the quality of applicants—that there was a shortage in the "social demand shortage" sense. The market for special education teachers was tighter than the markets for home care workers, pharmacists, and physical therapists, but even for that occupation, children with special needs were still being taught, albeit with less qualified teachers than might be desired (an issue that is examined in more detail below).

It was clear from both the literature and the interviews that what distinguishes labor markets today from those of our prior studies is the economy. The recession of 2008–2009 has been characterized as the worst recession since the Great Depression, and it is clear that the only period since 1948 with unemployment rates comparable to today's economy was in the 1982–1983 period. During that period, the unemployment rate was 10 percent or higher for 10 months, but in the 2008–2009 recession, there were only three months with an unemployment rate of at least 10 percent, and the peak rate was 10.1 percent compared to 10.8 percent in the earlier period.

A bad economy is likely to curtail occupational shortages for several reasons. First, the poor economy is likely to directly reduce demand for all types of labor because both families and government have less revenue to spend. On the supply side, workers are less likely to leave their current job during a recession for another job, possibly in another occupation, because they know or fear that few such opportunities are available. The JOLTS data track the quit rate from 2000 to 2010, and the data indicate that the monthly quit rate for all occupations dropped from a range of 1.8 to 2.5 percent from December 2000 to October 2008 to about 1.4 percent in recent months (BLS 2010e).

Although little evidence of occupational shortages was found, as noted in Chapter 2, there is evidence of use of potentially less productive individuals for special education positions, and this issue is discussed in the next section. In the other three occupations analyzed, there was no evidence of a decline in the quality of workers coming into the field.

For Policy Purposes It Is Important to Go Beyond an Economic Concept of a Shortage

The economic definition of an occupational shortage is of interest for economists trying to understand how markets work and why they sometimes fail, but the social demand shortage concept introduced by Arrow and Capron (1959) is also of interest for policy purposes. For three of the occupations studied—pharmacists, physical therapists, and home care workers—the market appears to be working reasonably well at this time. For special education teachers, however, the story is quite different. In this field, there has been a constant concern that there is a shortage of special education teachers. Cook and Boe (2007) trace the problem back to the passage of the Education of All Handicapped Children Act (now called the Individuals with Disabilities Education Act or IDEA) in 1975, which required states to implement policies to assure that children with disabilities receive a free and appropriate education.

Cook and Boe claim that the demand for special education teachers can be decomposed into quantity demand and quality demand. Interestingly, they conclude, "It is obvious that there has been, and likely will be, sufficient quantity supply of teachers to meet future quantity demand" (Cook and Boe 2007, p. 222). They go on to note that unless the teachers supplied are of adequate quality, "this is not an adequate solution." Cook and Boe conclude that entering special education teachers fall short of the quality desired because "only 46 percent of first-time [special education teachers] had both completed extensive teacher preparation specifically with degree majors in special education" (p. 224).

On the surface, the lack of specific special education teacher training sounds bad, but does this constitute a shortage? It is important to note here the differences between a purely private service, such as hair stylists, and workers who provide publicly supported services, such as teachers. If market conditions led to many poorly qualified hair stylists, economists would not consider this indicative of a shortage of stylists. But teachers are publicly supported, and public laws require that teachers have certain qualifications and, increasingly, that they be effective at teaching their students. Thus, although hiring less qualified teachers is a natural development in a tight labor market, it is only indicative of a shortage, in the economic sense, if the schools are failing to provide an education level mandated by law. In the case of special education teachers, it appears that this is not the case.

The NCLB legislation defines the concept of a "highly qualified teacher" as one with a bachelor's degree, full certification, and demonstrated expertise in the subject matter of each core subject taught (Boe 2006, p. 139). Moreover, Boe notes that the legislation requires that all public school teachers of core subjects be highly qualified, and he concludes, "Thus, there is a federal statutory quality demand for teachers who attain all three qualifications" (Boe 2006, p. 139). Boe measures the quality shortage of special education teachers by adding the number of vacant positions and the number of positions whose occupants are not fully certified. For the 1999–2000 school year, Boe estimates the quality shortage of special education teachers to be 13.7 percent for students aged 6 to 12, in contrast to a shortage of 10.5 percent for general education teachers.

Whether or not this situation constitutes a shortage in the economic sense depends on how the legal requirements of NCLB and IDEA are interpreted. Because schools appear to operate consistently without meeting the mandated requirements, one could argue that there is no economic shortage because the quality shortage appears to be a market solution that is tolerated. However, one could also argue that because the legal requirements of NCLB are not being met, there is a shortage in the economic sense.

Although it may be interesting for economists to argue about whether there is a shortage of special education teachers in the economic sense, it is more important to consider how the nation's children are affected by the fact that many special education teachers may not have the desired credentials. Of course, standards for teachers can be set too low even in the absence of a shortage, but in a tight labor market, schools are more likely to lower standards to make certain that someone is teaching the children. Setting standards for highly qualified teachers provides a mechanism to alert communities when their teachers do not measure up to certain standards.

Some Occupations with Tight Labor Markets Have Recently Increased Educational Standards

As previously discussed, employers frequently lower entry standards for workers during periods when there are tight labor markets. Such an approach is one way to attract more entrants to an occupation. Interestingly, two of the occupations analyzed, pharmacists and physical therapists, have increased the standards for entry in recent years, requiring entrants to the fields to obtain doctorate degrees. Schools of pharmacy only offered doctor of pharmacy (PharmD) degrees after 2003, and the APTA's Vision Sentence for Physical Therapy 2020 states, "By 2020, physical therapy will be provided by physical therapists who are doctors of physical therapy, recognized by consumers and other health care professionals as the practitioners of choice to whom consumers have direct access for the diagnosis of, interventions for, and prevention of impairments, functional limitations, and disabilities related to movement, function, and health" (APTA 2011c). Although the analysis conducted for this study did not indicate current shortages for the occupations, the labor markets for both pharmacists and physical therapists are currently fairly tight, and both occupations are judged to have had shortages in recent years.

There are several reasons why it may be advantageous to increase the educational preparation required for an occupation. Extending the preparation to the doctoral level provides entry-level practitioners with more thorough knowledge of the relevant theory and practice, and it permits workers in the occupation to gain experience and skills while in training rather than while in practice. In the case of physical therapists, an additional motivation for increasing the educational requirements is to increase the professional stature of physical therapists and permit physical therapists to have direct access to patients rather than work through physicians. In addition to the two occupations analyzed for this report that have recently increased educational requirements, there is an ongoing discussion in the field of nursing of phasing out the two-year associate degree in nursing and requiring registered nurses to obtain a bachelor's degree. Nursing has long been a field where the labor market has been tight, so it provides a third example of an occupation with a tight labor market where there may be an increase in the length of preparation time.

When an occupation is experiencing a shortage, however, increasing educational requirements can exacerbate the shortage. The greater expense and time required to qualify for the field may discourage some individuals from entering the field, although we have not seen evidence of this occurring in the occupations analyzed. Even if the supply of new workers is not reduced, extending the preparation period by a year will slow down the ability of an occupation to adjust to an increase in demand.

The decision on the length of preparation that should be required for an occupation is not a simple one, and there are many factors that should be considered. It is interesting, however, that in several instances there has been a strong interest in increasing preparation time when the occupation is experiencing a tight labor market or actual shortage.

UTILITY OF DATA USED TO ANALYZE OCCUPATIONAL SHORTAGES

As was discussed in Chapter 1, there is no simple way to determine if an occupation is experiencing a shortage, but obtaining certain information about the labor market for the occupation is essential. The BLS already collects a great deal of data on earnings and employment that can be used to help determine if there is a shortage or a tight labor market, and much of this information was presented in the case studies. Examples of this type of data include hourly wage rates, annual earnings, and unemployment rates for workers in the occupation. For assessing whether there is a shortage, it is useful to compare the occupation with similar occupations and other occupations or occupational groups that can serve as benchmarks, and to look at the data over a number of years to see if patterns have changed. Such data are available over many years, at the state and local level as well as nationally. In addition, the BLS produces projections of occupational employment for a 10-year horizon every two years, and although the projections data does not provide information about whether there is currently a shortage, it is useful for gauging whether a current shortage is likely to endure. The primary data not collected by the BLS, which are the most important data for assessing shortages, are job vacancy data by occupation.[5]

The same data that are useful for studying occupational labor shortages are also useful for important practical applications—providing labor market information for individuals engaged in career planning or job search and as input into government policies and decisions about immigration and temporary visa policies when these decisions are based on labor market conditions for specific occupations.

Individuals interested in career planning or job search are likely to access relevant information either directly from the BLS Internet site

(www.bls.gov) or by visiting state and local workforce investment programs, either in person at One-Stop Career Centers or electronically
through Internet sites maintained by states and local programs.[6] Of
course, there is a great deal of labor market information that can be useful for individuals interested in career planning and job search and that
is produced by the federal government, state and local governments,
and private parties. BLS publishes the *Occupational Outlook Handbook* every two years, and it provides descriptive information, data, and
projections for hundreds of occupations. Other BLS publications that
provide additional information are the *Occupational Outlook Quarterly*
and *Career Guide to Industries*.[7] The DOL's Employment and Training
Administration (ETA) is responsible for administering WIA and other
programs that serve workers, and ETA also provides resources to individuals interested in labor market information.[8]

As noted earlier, although the BLS does not collect job vacancy
data, about 15 states and roughly the same number of local areas do
conduct job vacancy surveys, as do a number of other countries. These
states collect the data, at their own expense, for a number of reasons.
Massachusetts, for example, offers five reasons why the state has gathered such data since 2002 (Massachusetts Department of Workforce
Development 2006): to 1) identify and respond to turning points in the
economy, 2) help analysts identify emerging labor and skill shortages,
3) design training programs that match the labor needs of the Massachusetts economy, 4) analyze labor needs and employment opportunities by economic region, and 5) determine which segments of the workforce are affected most adversely by economic changes.

Milwaukee, which was the first local area to collect job vacancy
data, gathers such data "to assess the number and type of jobs available
and the level of skill training employers need to fill openings" (University of Wisconsin–Milwaukee 2010).

States and local areas vary in the frequency with which they gather
job vacancy data. Some jurisdictions, such as Massachusetts, gather the
data twice per year, but others, such as Milwaukee, conduct annual surveys. Although semiannual surveys provide more current data, the costs
for data collection and analysis are much higher. Because of financial
pressure from the current recession, some states have cut back on their
efforts. For example, until recently, Jacksonville, Florida, contracted
with a private firm to conduct job vacancy surveys, but it no longer does

so. And Colorado now purchases data on help wanted on-line rather than conducting its own survey.

Although states and local areas suggest that they conduct the job vacancy surveys in part to learn about occupational labor shortages, the published reports generally avoid specific statements about when an occupation has a shortage. One state official suggested that a rule of thumb is that a vacancy rate of 5 percent or higher is interpreted as a shortage for the occupation, but his state did not have a formal definition of a shortage occupation. To indicate the severity of labor market problems, states and local areas also publish data on the number of workers per opening.

USING OCCUPATIONAL SHORTAGE DATA FOR IMMIGRATION AND TEMPORARY VISAS

Occupational shortage data can play an important role in the determination of which occupations are good candidates for admitting temporary or permanent foreign labor to fill vacancies. In this section, we describe the approach developed for the United States by Malcolm Cohen and the system currently used in the United Kingdom.

The DOL has retained Malcolm Cohen twice to develop approaches to use existing data to rank occupations as candidates for admission of foreign labor (Cohen 1990; Cohen and Schwartz 1982).[9] Cohen's approach is somewhat similar to the approach used in this report. However, the DOL wanted a quantitative ranking system based on regularly available data rather than a system that relied in part on interviews with knowledgeable parties. Cohen identified seven indicators of occupational shortages based on economic theory:[10]

1) Employment change in the recent past

2) Occupational unemployment rate in the recent past

3) Wage change in the recent past

4) Training required for the occupation

5) Replacement demand

6) Projected increase in occupational demand

7) Immigrants certified in the recent past

In his 1990 report, Cohen created an index of shortage by developing a seven-point scale for each indicator and summing the score of the seven indicators. Thus, an occupation could receive a score of between 7 and 49; in the 1990 study, the occupations with the tightest labor markets were for physical therapists and registered nurses, each of which scored 39. Although both of Cohen's reports were accepted by the DOL, it has never implemented the type of scheme he developed.

The United Kingdom, on the other hand, has implemented a system that makes use of comprehensive occupational shortage data and feedback from interested parties to identify shortage occupations that are eligible for immigration.[11] Under this system, the Migration Advisory Committee (MAC), which includes five economists and a representative of the UK Commission for Employment and Skills, makes recommendations to the government about which occupations are experiencing shortages. The MAC only deals with occupations with highly skilled workers (Tier 1) and skilled workers (Tier 2). To qualify for inclusion on the list, an occupation must be skilled, have a shortage, and be a "sensible" candidate for the list, and these three criteria are applied sequentially. The MAC uses both top-down and bottom-up approaches in its work, relying on labor market data from national surveys and presentations and meetings with stakeholders.

Once it is determined whether an occupation uses enough skills to qualify for Tier 1 or Tier 2, an assessment is made on whether the occupation is experiencing a shortage. The MAC uses the following 12 indicators in four broad categories to determine whether there is a shortage (Downs 2009):

Employer-Based Indicators
Skill shortage vacancies as a percentage of employment by
  occupation
Skill shortage vacancies as a percentage of all vacancies
Skill shortage vacancies as a percentage of hard-to-fill vacancies

Price-Based Indicators
Percentage change in median hourly pay for all employees
Percentage change in mean hourly pay for all employees

Relative premium to an occupation, given [skill level], controlling
for region and age

Volume-Based Indicators
Percentage change in unemployed by sought occupation
Percentage change in hours worked for full-time employees
Percentage change in employment
Absolute change in proportion of workers in occupation less than
one year

Indicators of Imbalance Based on Administrative Data
Absolute change in median vacancy duration
Stock of vacancies/claimant count by sought occupation

An occupation was considered to have a shortage if it exceeded the
threshold established for at least 50 percent of the indicators; because
there is no formulaic way to set the thresholds, they were established
judgmentally. The "sensible" criterion is by nature subjective and was
usually analyzed by using the bottom-up data provided by various
stakeholders.

The work done by Cohen (Cohen 1990; Cohen and Schwartz 1982)
in the United States and by the MAC in the United Kingdom indicates
that it is feasible to use labor market data to assist in the process of
determining shortages for admission of foreign workers on a temporary or permanent basis. Although Cohen (1990) developed a numerical
scale to rank occupations and the MAC approach also includes quantitative components, the flexibility of the MAC approach used has the
advantage of recognizing the lack of a clear measure of a shortage and
permitting qualitative data to be used in the process.

DEVELOPING BETTER OCCUPATIONAL SHORTAGE DATA
FOR THE UNITED STATES

Assessments of whether an occupation is experiencing a shortage can be made in the United States with available data. As stated
previously, Cohen (1990) developed seven indicators and suggested
aggregating them to rank occupations. Veneri (1999) uses employment

growth, increases in earnings, and occupational unemployment rates as indicators, but she suggests that case studies be conducted to add qualitative data to the assessment. The approach used in this study, and in the other shortage studies the authors have conducted, follows Veneri's suggestion. The United Kingdom also combines data from administrative sources and national surveys with data from various stakeholders, which is referred to as "bottom-up" information.

Although U.S. labor market data can be used to study occupational labor shortages, the data are not ideal for any of the purposes for which they are used—labor market information for job seekers and individuals conducting career exploration, labor market information for workforce investment programs such as WIA that need to know what training programs to make available to their customers, or for learning which occupations appear to have shortages. This is a difficult fiscal time for all levels of government, but good labor market information of all kinds can potentially provide significant benefits to youth exploring careers, job seekers, state and local workforce investment programs, employers, and federal officials trying to better understand and deal with the intertwined issues of occupational shortages and labor-related immigration and temporary visa programs. We suggest that the following actions be considered:

- **The BLS should give further consideration to expanding the JOLTS program to provide job vacancy data at the national level**. There is clearly strong demand for such data, as many states and local areas have voted with their pocketbooks to conduct their own surveys. Such data would be valuable for workforce investment programs, job seekers, policy officials, and researchers.

- **If the JOLTS program cannot be expanded, the BLS should explore the possibility of working with interested states and local areas in standardizing and possibly subsidizing job vacancy surveys**. There is already a loose consortium of states conducting these surveys, but the current economic and fiscal climate has led to at least one state abolishing its program. Only one of the 10 most populous states (Florida) has a statewide job vacancy program, so expanding the pool of participating states would require a great deal of effort to obtain a reasonable national picture.[12] However, if a national survey cannot be implemented, such a strategy might be a reasonable second-best strategy.

- **Job vacancy surveys should explore ways to obtain more detailed occupational data than that provided by the SOC codes**. As noted earlier in the report, although fine for many purposes, the SOC lacks sufficient detail in some instances to assess occupational shortages. This is not a simple problem to deal with—adding more occupations to the SOC is an expensive proposition. One possible solution would be to permit employers to define openings with more detail than the finest SOC level. Note that there are other dimensions to job characteristics that go beyond occupational descriptions that could lead to shortages even if there are people available in the occupation—pay and experience, for example.

- **If the data are improved, occupational shortage data should be systematically incorporated into the decision-making process for programs that admit foreign labor to the United States for programs such as H-1B visas and alien worker certification**. This project dealt only tangentially with these issues, but there is currently interest in reforming programs that admit foreign workers on a temporary or permanent basis to assure that such workers benefit the U.S. workforce rather than displace them.[13] Good occupational shortage data could greatly improve the quality of the decisions made.

- **Although currently available data can provide indicators of occupational shortages, much better determinations can be made with vacancy data and by including qualitative data gathered on a case-by-case basis**. Although levels and changes in data on labor market characteristics can be used to identify tight labor markets, or at least to identify increasing tightness in a labor market, all the theoretical studies and many of the applied studies point to the primary importance of job vacancy data as an indicator of a shortage. But job vacancy data are not sufficient to determine if there is an actual shortage or a tight labor market or if there is a shortage for some subcategory of the occupation. Veneri (1999) agrees with our conclusion here, and Downs (2009) documents how the "bottom-up" approach of gathering information from stakeholders is an important part of the United Kingdom's process for identifying occupational shortages.

Occupational labor shortages have been studied by economists since the 1950s. Much of the early work focused on specific occupations with rapidly growing demand. More recently, studies have analyzed other potential causes of shortages, such as government regulation of the labor market or the service produced. The topic is of greater interest than ever, given the increasingly sophisticated demands by workforce investment programs and job seekers, and the interest by many in seeing improvements in the process for assessing the need for foreign workers in the U.S. workforce. At the national level, the nation's labor statistics efforts have not kept up with the demand. A national system for collecting occupation-specific job vacancy data would be an important next step in improving our efforts in this area.

Notes

1. The unemployment rate was 6.9 percent for 1993 and 8.9 percent for 2011 (http://www.bls.gov/cps/cpsaat01.pdf, accessed June 12, 2012).
2. It is possible to obtain jobs listed with the state Employment Service agencies, but such lists are not exhaustive and are likely to be unrepresentative of all vacancies. Likewise, compilations of job openings posted on Internet sites or in newspaper want ads suffer from similar problems.
3. The Employment and Training Institute of the University of Wisconsin–Milwaukee has identified 15 states (Colorado, Connecticut, Florida, Kansas, Louisiana, Maine, Massachusetts, Minnesota, Nebraska, Nevada, New Jersey, Oklahoma, Rhode Island, Utah, and Washington) and 16 metropolitan or regional areas that conduct job vacancy surveys. The information is available at http://www4.uwm.edu/eti/pages/surveys/jos.htm (accessed August 17, 2010). The Institute also produced a manual on how to conduct such surveys (University of Wisconsin–Milwaukee 1998).
4. The BLS indicates that the 2010 SOC has 840 detailed occupations and 461 broad occupations (see http://www.bls.gov/SOC/#classification, accessed August 18, 2010).
5. As noted earlier, JOLTS does not produce vacancy data by occupation.
6. The Workforce Investment Act of 1998 (WIA) calls for the establishment of at least one comprehensive One-Stop Career Center in each of the more than 600 local workforce investment areas in the country, but in some areas workforce

services are also delivered at other locations such as local Employment Service offices or at satellite locations in places such as community colleges. Also, the One-Stops often have state or local brand names rather than being referred to as One-Stop Career Centers.

7. BLS publications and data on occupations are available at http://www.bls.gov/bls/occupation.htm (accessed August 21, 2010).

8. ETA publications, data, and information on programs and services can be found at http://www.doleta.gov/jobseekers/ (accessed August 21, 2010).

9. Cohen's work for the Department of Labor was later published as Cohen (1995).

10. In a presentation made at the symposium held in conjunction with this project, Cohen indicated that job vacancies would be a good measure if they were available (see http://epi.3cdn.net/85ec6cf493f0f84caf_36m6baufj.pdf, accessed August 21, 2010).

11. The description of the UK system is based on Downs (2009) and a presentation by Martin Ruhs at the symposium held for this project. The Ruhs presentation is available at http://epi.3cdn.net/7329ec8745d286ac32_zbm6b9nzz.pdf (accessed August 21, 2010).

12. State population data for 2009 were obtained at http://www.census.gov/popest/states/NST-ann-est.html, and a list of states with job vacancy surveys was from http://www4.uwm.edu/eti/pages/surveys/jos.htm (both accessed August 22, 2010).

13. There were several presentations on the issue of criteria for admitting foreign workers at the symposium cosponsored by the Economic Policy Institute and this project (see http://www.epi.org/publications/entry/event_20090520/, accessed August 22, 2010).

References

American Association of Colleges of Pharmacy (AACP). 2011. *Academic Pharmacy's Vital Statistics*. Alexandria, VA: AACP. http://www.aacp.org/about/Pages/Vitalstats.aspx (accessed September 22, 2011).

American Association for Employment in Education (AAEE). 2010. *Educator Supply and Demand in the United States*. Columbus, OH: AAEE. http://cst.cmich.edu/users/Franc1M/1esc400/Professional_Development_and_Jobs/job_prospects.pdf (accessed August 29, 2011).

American Physical Therapy Association (APTA). 2008. *Physical Therapy Workforce Project: Physical Therapy Vacancy and Turnover Rates in Acute Care Hospitals*. Alexandria, VA: APTA.

———. 2010a. *Physical Therapy Workforce Project: Physical Therapy Vacancy and Turnover Rates in Acute Care Hospitals*. Alexandria, VA: APTA.

———. 2010b. *Physical Therapy Workforce Project: Physical Therapy Vacancy and Turnover Rates in Outpatient Private Practices 2010*. Alexandria, VA: APTA.

———. 2011a. *Physical Therapist Member Demographic Profile 2010*. Alexandria, VA: APTA.

———. 2011b. *Physical Therapy Workforce Project: Physical Therapy Vacancy and Turnover Rates in Skilled Nursing Facilities 2011*. Alexandria, VA: APTA.

———. 2011c. *Vision 2020*. Alexandria, VA: APTA. http://www.apta.org/Vision2020/ (accessed April 15, 2012).

American Society of Health-System Pharmacists (ASHP). 2009. *2009 ASHP Pharmacy Staffing Survey Results*. Bethesda, MD: ASHP. http://www.ashp.org/DocLibrary/MemberCenter/SPPM/ASHP-Staffing-Survey2009.aspx (accessed June 20, 2011).

———. 2010. *2010 ASHP Pharmacy Staffing Survey Results*. Bethesda, MD: ASHP http://www.ashp.org/DocLibrary/MemberCenter/SPPM/2010-Staffing-Survey.aspx (accessed June 20, 2011).

Arrow, Kenneth J., and William M. Capron. 1959. "Dynamic Shortages and Price Rises: The Engineer-Scientist Case." *Quarterly Journal of Economics* 73(2): 292–308.

Barnow, Burt S. 1996. "The Economics of Occupational Labor Shortages." In *Handbook on Employment and the Elderly*, William Crown, ed. Westport, CT: Greenwood Publishing Group, pp. 349–373.

Barnow, Burt S., and D. Lee Bawden. 1991. *Skill Gaps in the Year 2000: A Review of the Literature*. Washington, DC: Urban Institute.

Barnow, Burt S., Amy B. Chasanov, and Abhay Pande. 1990. *Financial Incentives for Employer-Provided Training: A Review of Relevant Experience in the United States and Abroad.* Washington, DC: Urban Institute.

Benjamin, A. E., Ruth E. Matthias, Kathryn Kietzman, and Walter Furman. 2008. "Retention of Paid Related Caregivers: Who Stays and Who Leaves Home Care Careers?" *Gerontologist* 48(Special Issue 1): 104–113.

Bercovitz, Anita, Abigail Moss, Manisha Sengupta, Eunice Y. Park-Lee, Adrienne Jones, Lauren D. Harris-Kojetin, and Marie R. Squillace. 2011. *An Overview of Home Health Aides: United States 2007.* National Health Statistics Report No. 34. Hyattsville, MD: U.S. Department of Health and Human Services. http://www.cdc.gov/nchs/data/nhsr/nhsr034.pdf (accessed August 23, 2011).

Berman, Sheldon H., and David K. Urion. 2003. "The Misdiagnosis of Special Education Costs." *School Administrator* 60(3): 6–10.

Billingsley, Bonnie S. 2004. "Special Education Teacher Retention and Attrition: A Critical Analysis of the Research Literature." *Journal of Special Education* 38(1): 39–55.

———. 2005. *Cultivating and Keeping Committed Special Education Teachers: What Principals and District Leaders Can Do.* Thousand Oaks, CA: Corwin Press.

———. 2008. "Are You 'Highly Qualified' under IDEA 2004?" *Teaching LD.* http://www.teachingld.org/expert_connection/highly_qual.html (accessed August 15, 2010).

Birkeland, Sarah E., and Heather G. Peske. 2004. "Literature Review of Research on Alternative Certification." Washington, DC: National Education Association. http://www.teach-now.org/NEAFullText.pdf (accessed August 15, 2010).

Bishop, John H. 1996. "Is the Market for College Graduates Headed for a Bust? Demand and Supply Responses to Rising College Wage Premiums." *New England Economic Review* (May–June): 115–135.

Blank, David J., and George J. Stigler. 1957. *The Demand and Supply of Scientific Personnel.* New York: National Bureau of Economic Research.

Boe, Erling E. 2006. "Long-Term Trends in the National Demand, Supply, and Shortage of Special Education Teachers." *Journal of Special Education* 40(3): 138–150.

Boe, Erling E., and Lynn H. Cook. 2006. "The Chronic and Increasing Shortage of Fully Certified Teachers in Special and General Education." *Exceptional Children* 72(4): 443–460.

Boe, Erling E., Lynn H. Cook, Sharon A. Bobbitt, and Anita L. Weber. 1996. *Retention and Attrition of Teachers at the District Level: National Trends in Special and General Education.* Research Report 1996-TSD6. Philadelphia: University of Pennsylvania, Graduate School of Education, Center for Research and Evaluation in Social Policy. http://www.gse.upenn.edu/cresp/ pdfs/Turnover%20District%20Level%201996-TSD6.pdf (accessed March 21, 2012).

Boe, Erling E., Lynne H. Cook, and Robert J. Sunderland. 2008. "Teacher Turnover: Examining Exit Attrition, Teaching Area Transfer and School Migration." *Exceptional Children* 75(1): 7–31.

Brownell, Mary T., Paul T. Sindelair, Anne G. Bishop, Lisa K. Langley, and Seonjin Seo. 2002. "Special Education Teacher Supply and Teacher Quality: The Problems, the Solutions." *Focus on Exceptional Children* 35(2): 1–16.

Bureau of Labor Statistics. 2010a. *Occupational Outlook Handbook: 2010– 2011 Edition, Special Education.* Washington, DC: U.S. Department of Labor, Bureau of Labor Statistics.

———. 2010b. *Occupational Outlook Handbook: 2010–2011 Edition, Pharmacists.* Washington, DC: U.S. Department of Labor, Bureau of Labor Statistics. http://www.bls.gov/ooh/healthcare/pharmacists.htm (accessed July 26, 2012).

———. 2010c. *Occupational Outlook Handbook: 2010–2011 Edition, Physical Therapists.* Washington, DC: U.S. Department of Labor, Bureau of Labor Statistics. http://www.bls.gov/ooh/healthcare/physical-therapists.htm (accessed August 14, 2012).

———. 2010d. *Occupational Outlook Handbook: 2010–2011 Edition, Home Health and Personal Care Aides.* Washington, DC: U.S. Department of Labor, Bureau of Labor Statistics. http://www.bls.gov/ooh/healthcare/ home-health-and-personal-care-aides.htm (accessed July 26, 2012).

———. 2010e. *Job Openings and Labor Turnover Survey.* Washington, DC: U.S. Department of Labor, Bureau of Labor Statistics. http://data.bls .gov/PDQ/servlet/SurveyOutputServlet?data_tool=latest_numbers&series _id=JTS00000000QUR (accessed August 18, 2010).

———. 2011a. Occupational Employment Statistics (2006–2009 data). Washington, DC: U.S. Department of Labor, Bureau of Labor Statistics. http:// www.bls.gov/oes/oes_arch.htm (accessed August 28, 2011).

———. 2011b. *Occupational Employment and Wages News Release (2010 data).* Washington, DC: U.S. Department of Labor, Bureau of Labor Statistics. http://www.bls.gov/news.release/ocwage.htm (accessed August 28, 2011).

———. 2011c. *Occupational Employment Statistics.* Washington, DC: U.S. Department of Labor, Bureau of Labor Statistics. http://www.bls.gov/oes/ oes_data.htm (accessed June 30, 2011).

Burke, Gerald. 2005. "Skills Shortages: Concepts, Measurement, and Policy Responses." *Australian Bulletin of Labour* 31(1): 44–71.

Butz, William P., Gabrielle A. Bloom, Mihal E. Gross, Terrence K. Kelly, Aaron Kofner, and Helga E. Rippen. 2003. *Is There a Shortage of Scientists and Engineers? How Would We Know?* Santa Monica, CA: RAND Corporation.

Carlson, Elaine, Marsha Brauen, Sheri Klein, Karen Schroll, and Sharon Willig. 2002. "Study of Personnel Needs in Special Education: Key Findings." Washington, DC: U.S. Department of Education, Office of Special Education Programs. http://spense.education.ufl.edu/KeyFindings.pdf (accessed March 21, 2012).

Clark, Kelly A., and Rosemary Hyson. 2001. "New Tools for Labor Market Analysis: JOLTS." *Monthly Labor Review* 124(12): 32–37.

Cohen, Jordan L., Hugh F. Kabat, Mary Ann Koda-Kimble, Charles O. Rutledge, and Robert E. Smith. 2001. "Are We Delivering on Our Promise to Society to Assure the Safe Use of Medications? Educating Pharmacists to Continue Adding Value to Health Care." Report of the 2000–2001 Argus Commission. *American Journal of Pharmaceutical Education* 65(4): 6S–8S.

Cohen, Malcolm S. 1990. "Study on the Feasibility of Using Labor Market Information for Alien Certification Determination." Ann Arbor, MI: University of Michigan, Institute of Labor and Industrial Relations.

———. 1995. *Labor Shortages as America Approaches the Twenty-First Century.* Ann Arbor, MI: University of Michigan Press.

Cohen, Malcolm S., and Arthur R. Schwartz. 1982. "Methodology for Determining Whether There Are Sufficient Workers Available in Various Occupations—An Aid in the Certification of Immigrants." Ann Arbor, MI: University of Michigan, Institute of Labor and Industrial Relations.

Commission on Workforce Quality and Labor Market Efficiency. 1989. *Investing in People: A Strategy to Address America's Workforce Crisis.* Washington, DC: U.S. Department of Labor.

Cook, Lynn H., and Erling E. Boe. 2007. "National Trends in the Sources of Supply of Teachers in Special and General Education." *Teacher Education and Special Education* 30(4): 217–232.

Curran, B., and C. Abrahams. 2000. "Teacher Supply and Demand: Is There a Shortage?" Washington, DC: National Governors Association, Center for Best Practices. http://www.nga.org/cms/home/nga-center-for-best-practices/center-publications/page-archive/col2-content/title_teacher-supply-and-demand-is-there-a-shortage.html (accessed July 25, 2012).

Downs, Anna. 2009. "Identifying Shortage Occupations in the UK." *Economic and Labour Market Review* 3(5): 23–29.

Education Commission of the States. 2007. S*pecial Education Teacher Certification and Licensure—50 State Database.* Denver, CO: ECS. http://mb2

.ecs.org/reports/Reporttq.aspx?id=1542&map=0 (accessed July 26, 2012).

Ehrenberg, Ronald G., and Robert S. Smith. 2009. *Modern Labor Economics: Theory and Public Policy*. 10th ed. New York: Prentice Hall.

Feistritzer, C. Emily. 2005. "State Policy Trends for Alternative Routes to Teacher Certification: A Moving Target." Prepared for the "Conference on Alternative Certification: A Forum for Highlighting Rigorous Research," held in Washington, DC, September. http://www.teach-now.org/CEFState %20Overview%20FINAL4.pdf (accessed March 21, 2012).

———. 2006. *Alternative Teacher Certification: A State-by-State Analysis*. Washington, DC: National Center for Education Information.

Foundation for Hospice and Homecare. 2006. "Study Shows Home Health Care Workers Drive Nearly Five Billion Miles to Serve Elderly and Disabled Patients." Washington, DC: National Association for Home Care and Hospice. http://www.nahc.org/facts/homecareStudy.html (accessed July 25, 2012).

Fox News. 2007. "Autism Epidemic Follows Increase in Special Education Funding, Shift in Diagnosis." November 4. http://www.foxnews.com/story/ 0,2933,307997,00.html (accessed July 25, 2012).

Fraher, Erin P., Phillip Summers, Katie Gaul, and Stephen Rutledge. 2007. *Allied Health Job Vacancy Tracking Report*. Chapel Hill, NC: Cecil G. Sheps Center for Health Services Research, University of North Carolina at Chapel Hill. http://www.shepscenter.unc.edu/hp/publications/AHvacancy_ fall06.pdf (accessed November 28, 2012).

Franke, Walter, and Irving Sobel. 1970. *The Shortage of Skilled and Technical Workers*. Lexington, MA: Heath-Lexington Books.

Geiger, William L., Margaret D. Crutchfield, and Richard Maizner. 2003. "The Status of Licensure of Special Education Teachers in the 21st Century." COPSSE Document No. RS-7. Gainesville, FL: University of Florida, Center on Personnel Studies in Special Education. http://copsse.education.ufl .edu/docs/RS-7/1/RS-7.pdf (accessed March 21, 2012).

Giorgianni, Salvatore J. 2002. *Full Preparation: The Pfizer Guide to Careers in Pharmacy*. New York: Pfizer Pharmaceutical Group.

Green, Francis, Stephen Machin, and David Wilkinson. 1998. "The Meaning and Determinants of Skill Shortages." *Oxford Bulletin of Economics and Statistics* 60(2): 165–187.

Harrington, Paul E., and Andrew M. Sum. 1984. *Skills Shortages and Employment and Training Policy in the U.S.: Past Relationships and Desirable Future Directions*. Boston: Northeastern University, Center for Labor Market Studies.

Hecker, Daniel E. 1992. "Reconciling Conflicting Data on Jobs for College Graduates." *Monthly Labor Review* 115(7): 3–12.

Ingersoll, Richard M. 2001. "Teacher Turnover and Teacher Shortages: An Organizational Analysis." *American Education Research Journal* 38(3): 499–534.

Johnston, William B., and Arnold Packer. 1987. *Workforce 2000: Work and Workers in the Twenty-First Century.* Indianapolis, IN: Hudson Institute.

Kaiser Commission on Medicaid and the Uninsured. 2009. *Medicaid Home and Community-Based Service Programs: Data Update.* Washington, DC: Kaiser Family Foundation. http://www.kff.org/medicaid/upload/7720-03 .pdf (accessed July 25, 2012).

Kaiser Family Foundation. 2006. *Findings on Medicare Part D.* Menlo Park, CA: Kaiser Family Foundation.

———. 2008. *Prescription Drug Trends.* Menlo Park, CA: Henry J. Kaiser Family Foundation.

———. 2009. *Medicare Spending and Financing.* Menlo Park, CA: Henry J. Kaiser Family Foundation.

———. 2010a. *Prescription Drug Trends.* Menlo Park, CA: Henry J. Kaiser Family Foundation.

———. 2010b. *Medicaid and Long-Term Care Services and Supports.* Menlo Park, CA: Henry J. Kaiser Family Foundation. http://www.kff.org/medicaid/ upload/2186-07.pdf (accessed August 23, 2011).

———. 2010c. *The Medicaid Program at a Glance.* Menlo Park, CA: Henry J. Kaiser Family Foundation. http://www.kff.org/medicaid/upload/7235-04 .pdf (accessed August 23, 2011).

Katsiyannis, Antonis, Dalun Zhang, and Maureen A. Conroy. 2003. "Availability of Special Education Teachers: Trends and Issues." *Remedial and Special Education* 24(4): 246–253.

Langland, Connie. 2009. "Recruiting Special Education Teachers Proves to Be a Challenge for the District." *Focus on Teacher Excellence* 16(4). http:// www.thenotebook.org/summer-2009/091342/recruiting-special-education -teachers-proves-be-challenge-district (accessed March 21, 2012).

Levitan, Sar A., and Frank Gallo. 1989. "The Shortsighted Focus on Labor Shortages." *Challenge* 32(5): 28–32.

Markkaned, Pia, Margaret Quinn, Catherine Gallagin, Stephanie Chalupka, Letitia Davis, and Angela Laramie. 2007. "There's No Place Like Home: A Qualitative Study of the Working Conditions of Home Health Care Providers." *Journal of Occupational and Environmental Medicine* 49(3): 327–337.

Maryland Hospital Association. 2007. *MHA Hospital Personnel Survey Report, Calendar Year 2006.* Elkridge, MD: Maryland Hospital Association.

Massachusetts Department of Workforce Development. 2006. *Massachusetts Employment Projections through 2014.* Boston: Massachusetts Department of Workforce Development. http://lmi2.detma.org/Lmi/pdf/MEP2014.pdf (accessed August 15, 2010).

McLeskey, James, Naomi C. Tyler, and Susan Saunders Flippin. 2004. "The Supply and Demand for Special Education Teachers: A Review of Research Regarding the Nature of the Chronic Shortage of Special Education Teachers." *Journal of Special Education* 38(1): 5–22.

Montgomery, Rhonda J. V., Lyn Holley, Jerome Deichert, and Karl Kosloski. 2005. "A Profile of Home Care Workers from the 2000 Census: How It Changes What We Know." *Gerontologist* 45(5): 593–600.

Morvant, Martha, and Russell Gersten. 1995. *Attrition/Retention of Urban Special Education Teachers: Multi-Faceted Research and Strategic Action Planning*. Final Performance Report, Vol. 1. ERIC Document Reproduction Service No. 338 154. Eugene, OR: Eugene Research Institute.

Nakai, Karen, and Steve Turley. 2003. "Going the Alternate Route: Perceptions from Non-Credentialed Teachers." *Education* 123(3): 831–845.

National Association of Boards of Pharmacy (NABP). 2007. *Model State Pharmacy Act and Model Rules of the National Association of Boards of Pharmacy*. Mt. Prospect, IL: NABP.

National Association of Chain Drug Stores (NACDS). 2007. *The Chain Pharmacy Industry Profile*. Alexandria, VA: NACDS.

National Association for Home Care and Hospice (NAHC). 2009. *Home Care Aide National Certification Program*. Washington, DC: NAHC.

———. 2010. *Basic Statistics about Home Care*. Washington, DC: NAHC. http://www.nahc.org/facts/10HC_Stats.pdf (accessed August 23, 2011).

National Private Duty Association (NPDA). 2008. *State of Caregiving Industry Survey.* Indianapolis, IN: NPDA.

National Research Council (NRC). 2001. *Building a Workforce for the Information Economy*. Washington, DC: NRC, Committee on Workforce Needs.

———. 2007. *Building a Better NASA Workforce: Meeting the Workforce Needs for the National Vision for Space Exploration*. Washington, DC: NRC, Committee on Meeting the Workforce Needs for the National Vision for Space Exploration.

Palmer, Douglas J., and Robert Hall. 1987. "Teacher Training in Special Education." In *Encyclopedia of Special Education: A Reference for the Education of the Handicapped and Other Exceptional Children and Youth*, Cecil R. Reynolds and Lester Mann, eds. New York: John Wiley and Sons, p. 1478.

Rosenberg, Michael S., and Paul T. Sindelar. 2005. "The Proliferation of Alternative Routes to Certification in Special Education: A Critical Review of the Literature." *Journal of Special Education* 39(2): 117–127.

Sattler, Edward L., and Joan Sattler. 1985. "Economic Realities of Special Education." *Teacher Education and Special Education* 8(2): 98–103.

Scheckelhoff, Douglas. 2006. "2006 ASHP Pharmacy Staffing Survey Results." Bethesda, MD: American Society of Health-System Pharmacists.

Schommer, Jon C., Craig A. Penderson, Caroline A. Gaither, William A. Doucette, David H. Kreling, and David A. Mott. 2005. *Final Report of the National Sample Survey of the Pharmacist Workforce to Determine Contemporary Demographic and Practice Characteristics*. Madison, WI: Midwest Pharmacist Research Consortium.

Smith, Kristin. 2009. "Home Care Workers: Keeping Granite Staters in Their Home While They Age." New England Policy Brief No. 2. Durham, NH: University of New Hampshire, Carsey Institute. http://www.carseyinstitute .unh.edu/publications/PB_NH_HomeCare_09.pdf (accessed March 21, 2012).

Snyder, Thomas D., Alexandra G. Tan, and Charlene M. Hoffman. 2006. *Digest of Educational Statistics, 2005*. Washington, DC: National Center for Education Statistics, Institute of Education Sciences.

Stone, Robyn I. 2004. "The Direct Care Worker: The Third Rail of Home Care Policy." *Annual Review of Public Health* 25(3): 521–537.

Trutko, John, and Burt S. Barnow. 1998. *Workforce Requirements of the Shipbuilding Industry in Louisiana and Mississippi: Final Report*. Arlington, VA: James Bell Associates.

Trutko, John, Burt S. Barnow, Amy B. Chasanov, and Abhay Pande. 1993. *Labor Shortage Case Studies*. Research and Evaluation Report Series 93-E. Washington, DC: U.S. Department of Labor, Employment and Training Administration.

U.S. Department of Education. 2000. *History: Twenty-Five Years of Progress in Educating Children with Disabilities through IDEA*. Washington, DC: U.S. Department of Education.

———. 2002. *Study of Personnel Needs in Special Education*. Washington, DC: U.S. Department of Education.

———. 2002–2006. *Annual Report to Congress on the Implementation of the Individuals with Disabilities Education Act*. Washington, DC: U.S. Department of Education.

———. 2004a. *Twenty-Sixth Annual Report to Congress on the Implementation of the Individuals with Disabilities Education Act*. Washington, DC: U.S. Department of Education.

———. 2004b. *New No Child Left Behind Flexibility: Highly Qualified Teachers*. Washington, DC: U.S. Department of Education.

———. 2006. *Twenty-Eighth Annual Report to Congress on the Implementation of the Individuals with Disabilities Education Act*. Washington, DC: U.S. Department of Education.

————. 2007. *Questions and Answers on Highly Qualified Teachers Serving Children with Disabilities.* Washington, DC: U.S. Department of Education.

————. 2010. "U.S. Department of Education Launches National Teacher Recruitment Campaign." Press release, September 27. Washington, DC: U.S. Department of Education. http://www.ed.gov/news/press-releases/us-department-education-launches-national-teacher-recruitment-campaign (accessed July 26, 2012).

————. 2011. *Highly Qualified Teachers Revised State Plans.* Washington, DC: U.S. Department of Education. http://www2.ed.gov/programs/teacherqual/hqtplans/index.html (accessed July 26, 2012).

U.S. Department of Health and Human Services (DHHS). 1988. *Final Report.* Washington, DC: U.S. Department of Health and Human Services, Secretary's Commission on Nursing.

————. 2000. *The Pharmacist Workforce: A Study of the Supply and Demand for Pharmacists.* Washington, DC: U.S. Department of Health and Human Services, Health Resources and Services Administration.

————. 2003. *The Future Supply of Long-Term Care Workers in Relation to the Aging Baby Boom Generation: Report to Congress.* Washington, DC: U.S. Department of Health and Human Services, Administration on Aging.

————. 2007a. *National Health Expenditures Data.* Washington, DC: U.S. Department of Health and Human Services, Centers for Medicare and Medicaid Services.

————. 2007b. *Medicare and Home Health Care.* Washington, DC: U.S. Department of Health and Human Services, Centers for Medicare and Medicaid Services.

————. 2008a. *Medicare Modernization Update.* Washington, DC: U.S. Department of Health and Human Services, Centers for Medicare and Medicaid Services.

————. 2008b. *Medicare Prescription Drug Costs Continue to Drop.* Washington, DC: U. S. Department of Health and Human Services, Centers for Medicare and Medicaid Services.

————. 2008c. *Milestones of Drug Regulation in the United States.* Washington, DC: U.S. Department of Health and Human Services, Food and Drug Administration.

————. 2009a. *A Profile of Older Americans: 2009.* Washington, DC: U.S. Department of Health and Human Services, Administration on Aging.

————. 2009b. *National Health Expenditures Data NHE Web Tables.* Washington, DC: U. S. Department of Health and Human Services, Centers for Medicare and Medicaid Services. http://www.cms.gov/NationalHealthExpendData/02_NationalHealthAccountsHistorical.asp#TopOfPage (accessed July 1, 2011).

————. 2010. *A Profile of Older Americans: 2010.* Washington, DC: U.S. Department of Health and Human Services, Administration on Aging. http://www.aoa.gov/aoaroot/aging_statistics/Profile/2010/docs/2010profile.pdf (accessed July 5, 2011).

————. 2011. *Home Health Quality Initiative.* Washington, DC: U. S. Department of Health and Human Services, Centers for Medicare and Medicaid Services. https://www.cms.gov/homehealthqualityInits/ (accessed August 23, 2011).

University of Wisconsin–Milwaukee. 1998. *Surveying Job Vacancies in Local Labor Markets: A How-To Manual.* Milwaukee, WI: University of Wisconsin–Milwaukee, Employment and Training Institute. http://www4.uwm.edu/eti/manual.htm#issue1 (accessed August 21, 2010).

————. 2010. *Surveying Job Vacancies in Local Labor Markets: A How-to Manual.* Milwaukee, WI: University of Wisconsin–Milwaukee, Employment and Training Institute. http://www4.uwm.edu/eti/pages/surveys/jos.htm#other (accessed July 26, 2012).

Veneri, Carolyn M. 1999. "Can Occupational Labor Shortages Be Identified Using Available Data?" *Monthly Labor Review* 122(3): 15–21.

White, Sarah J. 2005. "Will There Be a Pharmacy Leadership Crisis? An ASHP Foundation Scholar-in-Residence Report." *American Journal of Health-System Pharmacy* 62(8): 845–855.

Wright, Bernadette. 2005. *Direct Care Workers in Long-Term Care.* Washington, DC: AARP Public Policy Institute.

Authors

Burt S. Barnow is the Amsterdam Professor of Public Service and of Economics at George Washington University. He received a BS in economics from the Massachusetts Institute of Technology and a PhD in economics from the University of Wisconsin–Madison. Prior to joining George Washington University, he was associate director for research at Johns Hopkins University's Institute for Policy Studies, where he worked for 18 years. Before that, he worked for eight years at the Lewin Group and for nearly nine years at the U.S. Department of Labor, including four years as director of the Office of Research and Evaluation in the Employment and Training Administration. As a labor economist, Barnow focuses much of his work on labor markets; over the years he has conducted a number of studies looking at whether particular labor markets have experienced shortages of workers and, if so, why. He has also conducted many studies of occupational training programs, including studies of how the programs are being implemented and how effective they have been. He teaches the core course on program evaluation and a doctoral program seminar on human capital. He has conducted evaluations of a variety of social programs, including job training, welfare, child support, and fatherhood programs.

John Trutko, president of Capital Research Corporation, has worked for more than 30 years as a policy analyst and program evaluation specialist. He has designed and managed many program evaluation studies and policy assessments, including a series of process and impact evaluations of federal and state workforce development initiatives. He has authored or coauthored over 75 reports for a wide variety of federal and state governments and foundations, including many reports for the U.S. Department of Labor. Trutko conducted his first study of labor shortages in the 1980s with Dr. Barnow and has continued to focus much of his research work over the past two decades on workforce development, training, and labor market issues. He holds a master's degree in economics from the University of Sussex in Brighton, England, and a bachelor's degree in political science from the University of Rochester.

Jaclyn Schede Piatak is a PhD candidate in public administration and policy at American University. Her research interests include public and nonprofit management, volunteering, philanthropy, and social policy. Her dissertation, "The Changing Face of Public Service: Understanding the Dedication, Altruism, and Career Choices of Government and Nonprofit Employees," examines what it means to be a public servant today by exploring differences in employee attitudes and behaviors across the government, nonprofit, and private sectors. She has a BA degree in political science from Providence College and an MA in public policy from Johns Hopkins University. Her professional experience includes five years with the Occupational Safety and Health Administration, U.S. Department of Labor, and a year with the Corporation for National and Community Service. She received the 2011 Charles H. Levine PhD Student Research Award from American University, as well as two awards for her work at the U.S. Department of Labor.

Index

The italic letters *f, n,* and *t* following a page number indicate that the subject information of the entry heading is within a figure, note, or table, respectively, on that page. Double letters, e.g., *nn,* indicate more than one such feature.

White workers, occupations of, 45, 114,
116*t*
WIA. *See* Workforce Investment Act
Wisconsin, special education teachers in,
51*t*, 52, 66, 76*t*
Women with infant children programs, as
long-term care recipients, 154
Work restructuring, as employer
adjustment, 21–22, 24, 26
Workforce, 1, 22
earnings for all, *vs.* case-studied
occupations, 53, 54*t*, 95, 95*t*,
123–125, 124*t*
employment for all, *vs.* case-studied
occupations, 46, 47*t*, 49–50, 49*t*,
90*t*, 91, 94, 94*t*, 118–120, 119*t*,
122, 123*t*, 145*t*, 146, 148, 148*t*
foreign labor in, 174–176, 178, 179
gaps in, and needs of employers, 1,
33*n*1, 148
qualified substitutes in, 13, 79, 81
recruitment of, 19–20
skill gap of, 1, 33*n*1, 186
slow labor market adjustment by,
29–30
supply and demand of, 3, 15, 25, 31,
33*n*3, 33*n*8, 50–52, 51*t*, 55–65
supply of women in, 149, 158
willingness of, 3–4, 135
Workforce Investment Act (WIA)
job training financed by, 23
labor-market data needed by, 177
One-Stop Career Centers under, 173,
179–180*n*6
Working conditions, 3, 147
administration paperwork as, 64, 82,
84, 98, 99–100
improvement of, as employer
adjustment, 24, 78, 79, 105–106,
148
as labor supply factor, 63–64, 66, 151,
156–157
Wyoming, special education teachers in,
50, 51*t*, 76*t*

Youth, as baby-bust generation in
workforce, 15

About the Institute

The W.E. Upjohn Institute for Employment Research is a nonprofit research organization devoted to finding and promoting solutions to employment-related problems at the national, state, and local levels. It is an activity of the W.E. Upjohn Unemployment Trustee Corporation, which was established in 1932 to administer a fund set aside by Dr. W.E. Upjohn, founder of The Upjohn Company, to seek ways to counteract the loss of employment income during economic downturns.

The Institute is funded largely by income from the W.E. Upjohn Unemployment Trust, supplemented by outside grants, contracts, and sales of publications. Activities of the Institute comprise the following elements: 1) a research program conducted by a resident staff of professional social scientists; 2) a competitive grant program, which expands and complements the internal research program by providing financial support to researchers outside the Institute; 3) a publications program, which provides the major vehicle for disseminating the research of staff and grantees, as well as other selected works in the field; and 4) an Employment Management Services division, which manages most of the publicly funded employment and training programs in the local area.

The broad objectives of the Institute's research, grant, and publication programs are to 1) promote scholarship and experimentation on issues of public and private employment and unemployment policy, and 2) make knowledge and scholarship relevant and useful to policymakers in their pursuit of solutions to employment and unemployment problems.

Current areas of concentration for these programs include causes, consequences, and measures to alleviate unemployment; social insurance and income maintenance programs; compensation; workforce quality; work arrangements; family labor issues; labor-management relations; and regional economic development and local labor markets.